USING AN
EMPLOYEE OWNERSHIP
TRUST
FOR BUSINESS TRANSITION

Anne-Claire Broughton • Courtney Kemp • Alison Lingane
Christopher Michael • Corey Rosen • Stacey Smith • Steve Virgil

The National Center for Employee Ownership
Visit us at **www.nceo.org** for more information about ESOPs

Using an Employee Ownership Trust for Business Transition

Anne-Claire Broughton, Courtney Kemp, Alison Lingane, Christopher Michael, Corey Rosen, Stacey Smith, and Steve Virgil

Book design by Scott Rodrick

First published in 2024

ISBN: 978-1-954990-35-7

The National Center for Employee Ownership
Phone (510) 208-1300
Website: www.nceo.org

Contents

Corey Rosen

EMPLOYEE OWNERSHIP TRUSTS (EOTs) are an increasingly common way for sellers of closely held companies to transition out of ownership. In an EOT, the company sets up a special-purpose trust to own shares that the company (not employees) buys from the seller using their future profits to repay a note, often from the seller or a combination of the seller and a bank. The trust is designed to hold the shares in perpetuity. The employees are generally not owners but have a claim on company profits through dividends or conventional profit shares. Companies could also add some form of equity grants to individuals.

EOTs are often chosen instead of an employee stock ownership plan (ESOP). An ESOP is a special form of employee ownership that offers sellers, employees, and companies substantial tax benefits. ESOPs are governed by the Employee Retirement Income Security Act of 1974 (ERISA) and, as such, are subject to a variety of legal requirements. That makes ESOP implementation and operation much more costly and complex than for EOTs. Sellers must decide whether these rules and costs justify an ESOP compared to the much less expensive and much more flexible EOT.

This book helps decision-makers decide whether an EOT is the right approach. Chapter 1 introduces EOTs and compares them with ESOPs. Chapter 2 elaborates on how EOTs work, and chapter 3 delves into structuring them. Chapter 4 explores EOT financing, while chapter 5 discusses EOT governance. Chapter 6 discusses how EOTs can share equity rights with employees. Finally, chapter 7 provides case studies of EOT companies. Feedback and questions are very welcome; send them to me at crosen@nceo.org.

CHAPTER 1

How ESOPs Compare to EOTs

Corey Rosen

$\mathcal{M}$OST BUSINESS OWNERS who end up selling to an employee ownership trust (EOT) also consider selling to an employee stock ownership plan (ESOP), ultimately deciding that the costs, complexity, or rules for ESOPs are not worth the tax benefits that only ESOPs can provide. This chapter provides a basic look at how ESOPs work and then concludes with an extensive table comparing the pros and cons of ESOPs and EOTs.

How ESOPs Work

An ESOP is a kind of employee benefit plan, similar in many ways to qualified retirement plans such as 401(k)s and governed by the same laws: the Internal Revenue Code (the "Code") and the Employee Retirement Income Security Act of 1974 (ERISA). ESOPs are funded by the employer, not the employees. Participants are employees meeting minimum service requirements; company stock is held for them in a trust and allocated based on relative pay or a more level formula, then distributed after the employee terminates. ESOPs cannot be used to share ownership only with select employees, nor can allocations be made on a discretionary basis.

For the employees, no contributions are required to purchase the owner's shares. The owner can stay with the business in whatever capacity is desired. The plan is governed by a trustee who votes the shares, but the board appoints the trustee, so changes in corporate control are usually nominal unless the plan is set up by the company to give employees more input at this level.

Benefits for Selling Owners

ESOPs can be a very attractive and tax-favored way to sell a business. For the owner of a C corporation selling to an ESOP that will own 30% or more of the stock after the sale, taxation on the gain from the sale proceeds can be indefinitely tax-deferred by electing "rollover" treatment under Code Section 1042. The seller elects the deferral and reinvests (rolls over) the sale proceeds or an equivalent amount in the securities of other domestic companies (other than real estate trusts, mutual funds, and other passive investments) during the period starting three months before the sale and ending twelve months afterward. If these securities are not sold before the owner's death, no capital gains tax is ever due. If some of the reinvested securities are sold before death, tax is due only on a prorated basis. If the company is an S corporation, LLC, or partnership, it can convert to a C corporation before the sale so the seller can take advantage of this tax deferral. (This tax incentive is not available for S corporation owners.)

Another benefit for owners selling to an ESOP is that the sale can be all at once or gradual, for as little or as much of the stock as desired, allowing the seller to make a gradual transition if desired. In contrast, outside buyers often want to purchase the entire company in a single transaction, often imposing contingencies such as earn-out provisions that adjust installment payments to the seller based on how the company performs after the sale. Sales to EOTs also can be structured as a partial or total sale. The EOT could buy part of the company while the existing owners retain the rest, or the EOT could buy a partial interest while an ESOP or employees individually buy the remaining shares. As long as the EOT is the majority owner, the company can be set up so that it is not meant to be sold.

If the company remains an S corporation, the owner must pay capital gains tax on the sale, but all the other benefits of selling to an

ESOP remain. The most important of these is that the owner's shares are bought in tax-deductible dollars, either from company contributions or plan borrowings.[1]

Financing an ESOP

The simplest way to finance an ESOP to transfer ownership is to have the company make tax-deductible cash contributions to the ESOP trust, which the trust then uses to gradually purchase the owner's shares. Alternatively, the owner can have the ESOP borrow the funds needed to buy the shares. In this way, larger amounts of stock can be purchased all at once, up to 100% of the equity. The loan is made to the company (the external loan), which then reloans the money to ESOP (the internal loan). The external loan is usually paid off in five to seven years; the internal loan is paid off more slowly because the payment of that loan releases shares to the employee accounts, and by extending the internal loan, the shares can be released to current and future employees more gradually.

Typically, the bank will loan a company only enough to buy a portion of the total shares, often around 30% to 50%. The bank may also want a personal guarantee if company collateral is insufficient. The guarantee is often in the form of the investments the seller purchases with the gains from the sale.

Many, and probably most, ESOPs are funded at least in part by a seller note. The seller note can fund the purchase of shares the bank loan does not cover, or it can be used for the entire sale. The ESOP acquires the shares and then pays back the seller at a reasonable rate of interest (not more than what a commercial lender would charge for loans of similar risk). Sellers often like this idea because they not only sell their shares but also get a reasonably good rate of return on the note. In this scenario, however, recall that for a seller to elect the

---

1. Net interest deductions for businesses with more than $30 million in average annual revenue (as of 2024, as indexed for inflation) are limited to 30% of adjusted taxable income (similar to EBIT (earnings before interest and taxes]), although this is not an issue for 100% ESOP-owned S corporations because they pay no taxes.

Section 1042 tax-deferred rollover, the window for reinvesting the proceeds ends 12 months after the sale. Hence, the seller can reinvest all of the sale proceeds only if they have other funds available or, as normally happens, they borrow money from a bank to buy special ESOP investments that qualify for this kind of sale (an increasingly common approach). The seller then repays the banks with the proceeds of the note. However the money is obtained, the price the ESOP pays the selling owner for the stock is set by an independent appraiser, as discussed below.

Selling to an ESOP Versus a Redemption or Sale to Another Firm

Compare the ESOP buyout to two other common methods of selling an owner's shares: redemption or sale to another firm. Under a re-demption, the company gradually repurchases the shares of an owner. Corporate funds used to do this are not deductible.[2] A $3 million purchase in a redemption would normally require over $4 million in profits to fund once taxes are paid. Moreover, the owner must pay tax on the gain, at capital gains or dividend rates. In a sale to a C corpora-tion ESOP, the money made is considered a capital gain, not ordinary income, and the seller can indefinitely defer taxes on the proceeds if the seller qualifies for and elects Section 1042 rollover treatment, as discussed above. Even more important, the company only needs $3 million to fund the $3 million purchase, which also applies to sales to ESOPs in S corporations. Or consider the second alternative, selling to another company or individual. In a cash sale, taxes would be due immediately. If the sale is for an exchange of stock in the acquiring company, taxes can be deferred until the new stock is sold, but 80% of the company must be sold all at once, and the owner ends up with an undiversified investment for retirement.

---

2. See note 1 above regarding limits on interest deductions for larger companies.

S Corporation ESOPs

If a company is an S corporation, the profits attributable to the ESOP are not taxable. So if the ESOP is a 30% owner, income taxes are not due on 30% of the profits; if it is a 100% owner, no taxes are due, a rule that has led to the rapid growth of 100% S corporation ESOPs, often conversions from C corporation companies with ESOPs after they make the final purchase of shares.

Many companies convert to S status from C after the seller elects the tax-deferred Section 1042 rollover. If the company was an S corporation before converting to C status to enable the seller to get a tax deferral, it must wait five years before reconverting to S. If the company is an S and stays S, the tax benefits can make selling to an ESOP less expensive. Say the ESOP owns 30% of the stock. The company makes $1 million and distributes $210,000 to the 70% owners to pay their personal income tax obligation on the $700,000 in profits attributable to them. Under S corporation rules, distributions must be made pro-rata to the ownership share, so the ESOP gets $90,000, even though it pays no taxes. It can retain this cash each year to make a large stock purchase, or it can use it annually for smaller purchases. In effect, the company is buying shares from one or more non-ESOP owners with money that would have been used to pay taxes.

How the Price the Selling Owner Receives Is Determined

The price the ESOP will pay for the shares, as well as any other purchases by the plan, must be determined at least annually by an outside, independent appraiser. The appraiser's valuation is based on several factors. Most appraisers try first to find comparable public companies and use their price/earnings ratio, price/assets ratio, and other guides for setting a price. Discounted cash flow, book value, the company's reputation, future market considerations, and other factors are considered as well. The appraiser will try, as much as possible, to determine how much the business would be worth if there were a market for it. The appraiser is assessing what a financial buyer would pay, one who would operate the business as a standalone entity. A strategic buyer, such as a competitor, by contrast, might pay an additional premium because when the target company is acquired, there are perceived operational synergies that make the target more profitable to the buyer than it would be as a standalone entity. The ESOP cannot match this price because it cannot generate these synergies. Sales to synergistic buyers do trigger capital gains taxes, however, and often come with numerous contingencies.

How Employees Get Stock

ESOPs are much like other tax-qualified retirement plans. At least all employees who have worked at least 1,000 hours in a plan year must be included. They receive allocations of shares in the ESOP based on relative pay or a more level formula. If there is an ESOP loan, the shares are allocated each year based on the percentage of the loan that is repaid that year. The allocations are subject to vesting for as long as six years. Employees do not receive a distribution of shares until they terminate, and then the distribution can be delayed for five years if for reasons other than death, retirement, or disability. The plan is governed by a trustee appointed by the board; employees only have very limited required voting rights (they do not have to elect the board, for instance), although companies may provide additional rights.

It is important to understand that ESOPs do not allow employers to pick and choose who can get stock or to make allocations based on discretionary decisions. It is also critical to remember that ESOPs do not entail employees using their own money to buy shares. The company funds the plan. The ESOP trust holds the shares, and the ESOP trustee is the shareholder of record for the company stock in the plan; the participants are beneficial owners who have accounts in the ESOP.

Costs and Complexity

With all these benefits come very specific rules and requirements. That, in turn, makes setting up an ESOP much more costly and less flexible than an EOT. Whereas an EOT can generally be set up for $50,000 to

$100,000, ESOP startup costs usually range from $150,000 to $500,000 (or more in very large and complex deals). These costs may be well worth it given the tax benefits of an ESOP, but not for every company, and especially not for smaller companies. ESOPs generally work best for profitable companies with at least 20 employees. Ongoing ESOP costs are far lower, usually around $30,000 annually for most ESOPs, and increase with company size. Ongoing EOT costs are minimal.

Sales to an ESOP involve multiple players, including an ESOP attorney, corporate attorney, appraiser, outside trustee for the transaction, and, in larger deals, someone who can help locate non-bank financing. EOTs usually just have an attorney and an appraiser, although an appraiser, while recommended, is not required. On an ongoing basis, ESOPs must have a trustee (internal or external) to make sure the required annual appraisal is done properly and that the plan otherwise follows the law. EOTs do not have this requirement for an annual appraisal. Some owners also do not like the rules for ESOPs, such as the required formulas for who is in the plan and how much they get. EOTs have no rules about eligibility, allocation, and vesting other than those the owner or board set.

ESOP companies can also be required to sell if a buyer offers a very high premium (usually at least 50% above fair market value or more). That is because the ESOP operates under retirement plan rules that require the trustee to maximize the value of plan assets and pay no attention to the impact of a sale on employment issues. In practice, ESOP companies can make themselves very unappealing to acquire, so these forced sales are very rare, but an EOT can write rules into the trust to completely preclude this issue.

Is It Really Ownership?

Finally, unlike ESOPs, EOTs usually do not provide any claim on equity to employees, although they can be set up that way. ESOPs, by definition, do provide a claim on equity. Sellers need to decide how important ownership is in making a choice. As owners, employees may have a longer-term focus than when they only share profits. On the other hand, ESOP companies have to repurchase the shares from employees at some point, creating a financial obligation an EOT does not have.

Making the Decision: ESOP vs. EOT

All of this may sound appealing, but it is not feasible for every company. Several factors must, at a minimum, be present:

1. *The company is making enough money to buy out an owner.* The company must generate enough cash to buy the shares, conduct its normal business, and make necessary reinvestments.

2. *Payroll must be adequate to cover the purchase.* Because there are some limits (albeit generous ones) on how much can go into the ESOP each year, if a business has an exceptionally high value relative to its payroll, it may not be a good ESOP candidate, although this is an unusual scenario.

3. *If the company is borrowing to buy the shares, its existing debt must not prevent it from taking out an adequate loan.* Similarly, the company must not have bonding covenants or other agreements that prohibit it from taking on additional debt.

4. *If the seller wants to take the tax-deferred Section 1042 rollover, the company must be a regular C corporation or convert from S to C status.* S corporations can establish ESOPs, but their owners cannot take advantage of the tax-deferred rollover described above.

5. *The seller(s) must be willing to sell their shares at fair market value, even if the ESOP pays less than an outside buyer would.* An ESOP will pay the appraised fair market value based on a variety of factors, but sometimes an outside buyer can pay more for a company if it has a particular fit that creates synergies that go beyond what the company is worth on its own.

6. *Management continuity must be provided.* Banks, suppliers, and customers will all want to be persuaded that the company can continue to operate successfully. It is essential that people be trained to take the place of departing owners to ensure a smooth transition.

Summary: ESOPs vs. EOTs

The tax benefits for ESOPs are substantial and not available to EOTs, but the costs, rules, and complexity of an ESOP make them not the right choice for every owner. EOTs can provide a practical alternative. Table 1-1 summarizes the key differences between EOTs and ESOPs.

Table 1-1. ESOPs versus EOTs		
	Form of employee ownership	
	ESOPs	EOTs
What kinds of companies typically use these plans?	Established companies with owners seeking a partial or complete ownership transition. A minority of plans are used by companies simply to share the wealth employees help create. Companies must be C corporations, S corporations, or LLCs taxed as a C or S corporation.	Companies seeking a business transition that want legal protection for preserving their legacy, community benefit, for social and environmental goals, or that do not want to comply with the rules and costs of an ESOP and are willing to trade off the tax benefits of ESOPs to do so. Trusts can be designed to be permanent to prevent a sale to another buyer, something that may not be possible in an ESOP.
Primary uses	1. To be a new owner of the business, often when the current owner wants to retire. 2. Providing incentives and rewards broadly to the workforce.	1. Preserving the culture, protecting the workforce, or maintaining a values-based decision-making process. 2. Business transitions in closely held companies.
Tax benefits to owners of companies	1. Sellers can defer capital gains taxes on a sale to ESOP if the sale meets certain requirements. 2. The purchase of shares by the ESOP can be funded with pretax dollars out of future profits. Stock redemptions outside of ESOPs must be funded with after-tax dollars.	None

Table 1-1. ESOPs versus EOTs		
Form of employee ownership		
	ESOPs	EOTs
Tax treatment for companies	1. Contributions to an ESOP are tax-deductible, including both principal and interest, when repaying a loan to the ESOP to purchase shares. 2. The profits attributable to the ESOP trust in an S corporation ESOP are not taxable. 100% ESOP-owned S corporations thus pay no income tax.	EOT companies often pay profit sharing to employees, which is a deductible expense. Contributions to the employee ownership trust may be tax-deductible to the company.
Tax treatment for employees	ESOPs are taxed the same way as other tax-qualified retirement plans are. Employees pay no tax on the contributions to the trust until they receive a distribution of their account balances, generally after termination of employment. Taxes can be further deferred on any amount rolled into another retirement account, usually an IRA.	EOTs often pay annual profit sharing, which is taxable to employees the same way a bonus is, i.e., subject to payroll taxes.
Who must be included in the plan	Generally, at least all employees who work 1,000 or more hours in a plan year, have a year of service, and are aged 21 or older. Companies may choose to include employees earlier. Some segments of the workforce may be excluded.	Companies can choose which employees they want to include, but most EOTs include most or all employees.

Table 1-1. ESOPs versus EOTs		
	Form of employee ownership	
	ESOPs	EOTs
How are equity allocations determined?	Employees get an allocation of annual company contributions to the plan based on their relative compensation among eligible employees or a more level formula. Pay over a certain amount ($345,000 as of 2024, indexed annually) does not count.	Companies choose their own formulas for profit sharing. The EOT, not the individual employees, owns the shares. If the company is sold, any equity value is generally divided between employees there at the time of the sale, based on a formula the company determines. Companies can choose to set up some kind of equity-sharing plan, such as stock options, restricted stock, or synthetic equity, in addition to the EOT.
When do equity allocations become non-forfeitable (vest)?	Vesting must start no later than after the second year of service. A year of service is a plan year with 1,000 hours of service or, if the company chooses, a smaller number.	Because there are no actual equity allocations, vesting is not an issue.
When do employees get paid for their ownership share?	Distribution of employee account balances generally must start no later than five years after the end of the plan year except for terminations due to death, disability, and retirement, in which case distribution must start no later than one year after the end of the plan year.	Employees normally receive profit shares from the company.

Table 1-1. ESOPs versus EOTs		
	Form of employee ownership	
	ESOPs	EOTs
Governance	The ESOP trust is the legal shareholder. The trustee is appointed by the board. The trustee votes the shares. Employees have limited voting rights unless the company chooses to provide greater rights.	Companies can choose the control rights the trust exercises and whether employees have any say. The seller generally determines the purpose under which the trust must operate and what role the employees have in governing the trust. Most trusts are designed to be permanent, however, so that the company is not sold.
Valuation	The ESOP trust cannot pay more than fair market value, defined as what a willing financial buyer would pay for the percentage of the company the ESOP trust is purchasing. The trustee hires the appraisal firm. Appraisals must be done annually. ESOPs generally can pay what most other financial buyers would pay, but about 10% to 20% of potential sellers to ESOPs could get a substantial premium by selling to a synergistic buyer.	There are no rules for how shares are appraised, although a valuation is advisable.
Fiduciary issues	The ESOP trustee is responsible for assuring that the plan is operated in the best interest of plan participants. This includes making sure the appraisal is done properly and that the plan operates within its rules and the requirements of the law.	Fiduciary issues depend on the state law governing the trust.

Table 1-1. ESOPs versus EOTs		
	Form of employee ownership	
	ESOPs	EOTs
Costs	ESOPs generally cost between $150,000 and $300,000 to set up but can cost more in larger and complex deals. Nonleveraged ESOPs have much lower setup costs. Costs are generally less than the costs of selling to a third party. Ongoing costs are about $20,000 to $30,000 annually for most ESOPs, with costs going up with size.	Initial costs are generally from $30,000 to $100,000; ongoing costs are not significant.
Financing	ESOPs are paid for by the company, not the employee. ESOPs can be financed by annual cash contributions to the plan in a gradual sale or by leverage when the ESOP buys more up front. ESOP loans can come from seller notes, banks, and/or mezzanine lenders.	The trust is funded by the company.
Complexity	ESOPs are subject to detailed federal rules and require that the company devote internal resources to compliance. Setting up an ESOP is similarly more complicated than other employee ownership plans but less complicated than a sale to another company.	Because EOTs are not covered by any specific set of rules, they are less complicated and more flexible than ESOPs to set up and administer.

Table 1-1. ESOPs versus EOTs		
	Form of employee ownership	
	ESOPs	**EOTs**
When these plans do not fit	1. Because of their initial costs, ESOPs generally do not work for companies with fewer than 15 to 20 employees. 2. Good candidates for ESOPs need to have successor management in place if the seller is a key corporate officer. 3. Companies must have sufficient profitability to pay the added non-productive expense of buying out one or more owners. 4. Companies must be comfortable with the idea of most employees owning shares. While ESOPs can provide additional equity outside the plan to selected individuals, they cannot base awards on discretionary decisions.	Companies looking for tax-favored means of providing liquidity are not good fits for EOTs.

CHAPTER 2

A Simpler Path Toward Employee Ownership: Key EOT Benefits

Christopher Michael

NTREPRENEURS ARE ARTISTS. They take the raw ingredients of vision and passion and, by investing their blood, sweat, and tears, create a venture that is unique and personal to them. Unsurprisingly, we often hear entrepreneurs refer to their business as their "baby." Entrepreneurs also worry about what will happen to their creations when they retire or walk away—especially if they don't have a succession plan. For instance, if a qualified family member is not ready and able to take over, an owner faces a tough choice: to sell or not to sell.

Opting to sell a business can be difficult for any entrepreneur. It's a very personal decision. For older business owners, selling also comes with long-term financial implications. For most entrepreneurs, their business is the most valuable asset in their financial portfolio. So, if the time comes to sell the business, it becomes imperative to understand the long-term implications of such a decision.

If the entrepreneur chooses to sell to a private equity firm or a competitor, what will happen to the culture of the business? Will the loyal employees who helped build the business be fairly rewarded for their contributions under new ownership? Will the culture of the business survive? Will the business even be recognizable for what it was? It's a lot to wrestle with.

That's why more and more entrepreneurs interested in preserving the legacy and the long-term impact of their businesses—while also making a win-win financial deal—are exploring the growing field of employee ownership as their succession plan. The idea is that by selling the business to its employees, the company founder can take some financial chips off the table while preserving everything that makes the business a special place to work for its employees. But how can an owner make this transition as simply, efficiently, and economically as possible?

Employee ownership trusts (EOTs), have emerged as an increasingly viable option for entrepreneurs to help create and sustain employee-owned businesses into the future without the need to make financial sacrifices or cede control of the company's legacy.

Trust Ownership

EOTs use the perpetual purpose trust form of ownership. Such a trust can exist without beneficiaries. Its purpose is specifically to create employee ownership. With an EOT, a trustee holds the company stock on behalf of most or all employees.

While somewhat overlooked, EOTs have been around for some time. A version of the EOT was deployed in the U.S. as early as 1897 in Washington State. The Columbia Conserve Company also embraced an early version of an EOT in 1926. But, until recently, EOTs have been much more popular in the United Kingdom, where generations of companies have followed the lead of the John Lewis Partnership, a popular retailer with some 89,000 employees that has had an EOT since 1929.

The lack of examples of prominent EOTs in the U.S. helps explain why, when most entrepreneurs begin their research into employee ownership, they first learn about employee stock ownership plans (ESOPs). Championed by Louis Kelso starting in the 1950s and given preferential tax status in 1974 under the Employee Retirement Income Security Act (ERISA), ESOPs have given employees an ownership opportunity at tens of thousands of companies.

An ESOP is a tax-qualified *retirement plan* that acquires shares of a company and then credits those shares to *individual employee accounts*. ESOPs can be amazing engines for generating retirement wealth for their participants, giving them a stake in helping to grow the value of their company. As the value of the business grows, so does the value of an employee's share in the ESOP. There are several examples of ESOPs where their employee-owners have retired as millionaires.

However, ESOPs have barriers to overcome in how business owners perceive them. Fairly or not, ESOPs have developed a reputation as complex and expensive to install, manage, and sustain for the long term. Entrepreneurs are often told that their business is too small, or sometimes even too large, to consider embracing an ESOP. There's also the constant presence of regulatory forces and "red tape" under the Department of Labor, the Internal Revenue Code, and ERISA that keep ESOPs on their toes, including the requirement to conduct an independent valuation of the business every year (unless it is a public company). And, if long-term employee ownership is the goal, ESOPs may not achieve the intended outcome due to the possibility of a forced sale——even when the founders and employees don't want it.

This context helps to explain why more and more business owners are rediscovering EOTs as a viable alternative for creating a sustainable employee-owned company.

Streamlining the Transaction

An EOT differs from an ESOP in one primary way: *an EOT is not a retirement plan*. While ESOP participants enjoy the benefit of seeing their accounts grow over the time they work for their employer, they won't fully realize the fruits of their labor until some time after they leave their jobs or retire due to legal rules. However, *in EOTs, employees receive financial rewards, typically through a profit-sharing plan, while working at the company*. At the same time, nothing prevents an EOT company's board of directors from using a portion of the surplus available to the company in any given year for additional employer contributions to an ERISA-based plan, such as a 401(k) plan.

An EOT conveys ownership in the company to employees, just as an ESOP does. However, there is typically no equity component (no individual employee share accounts) with an EOT. The standard practice is that when employees leave the company, they do not receive any compensation relative to the value of the company. As is said in the United Kingdom, participants in an EOT are "naked in, naked out." This means that employees do not buy into the plan when they enter the company and are not bought out when they leave. This is just the same as in any professional partnership, like a law firm, architectural firm, or medical practice. In some cases, a nominal buy-in and fixed buyout might be involved in such a firm. But the main benefit of participating in such a professional partnership is to participate in the profits, not the equity growth of the firm.

In a broader sense, EOTs offer five significant advantages for any entrepreneur looking to streamline the transition to an employee-owned company: privacy, flexibility, low cost, simplicity, and sustainability.

1. Privacy

Many, if not most, entrepreneurs value confidentiality and privacy. They're not interested in anyone beyond their accountant digging into their company's books. How much profit the business makes, or what investments the owner makes, is nobody's business but their own. Businesses are, after all, generally *private concerns*. Our entire economic and legal system is premised on this notion. Of course, public companies are another beast altogether. But when a private business owner considers employee ownership as a succession plan, they need to think about the repercussions of that decision. If a business owner sells to an ESOP or even a large private equity firm, they are engaging in a transaction in which many people will see their financials. Due to the transparent nature of the transaction, they'll need to bring in a host of experts for help and guidance, including investment bankers, lawyers, appraisers, a trustee, and accountants. It's not an exaggeration to note that, during such a quasi-public transaction, an owner might find that three dozen people or more are scrutinizing their company's financials or the transaction's details.

With an EOT sale, there may be only one outside party involved: the advisor you hire to structure the deal. Not only does this help ensure maximum privacy, but, more importantly, it also helps speed up the transaction's pace, which is often another big plus for business owners. Further, due to the internal and private nature of an EOT sale, the seller may reduce the potential for litigation over how the business was valued and how the final sale price was calculated after earnouts, performance targets, and other variable measures of the firm's value.

Of course, business owners should rely on the standing counsel of their firm's accountant and lawyer, just as with any other major transaction. And a business selling to an EOT may choose to seek an outside appraisal. Moreover, if bank financing is sought, then a commercial bank would naturally be involved in the transaction. That said, as with ESOPs and management buyouts, EOT deals are often structured with seller financing. This typically involves the selling owner taking a promissory note with principal and interest payments paid over several years. It may also involve warrants, which function like stock options, allowing a selling owner to take a "second bite at the apple." Seller financing shortens the time frame for closing the transaction and helps to further alleviate privacy concerns the seller might have with bringing on additional eyes to vet the company's financials.

2. Flexibility

An EOT provides owners with a great deal of latitude in structuring the trust, provided that the business follows international ethical principles for employee ownership. For example, if a business owner is concerned about the business sustaining its environmental or social impact after they are gone, customized rules can be written into the trust as a secondary purpose of the trust. For that matter, the trust may also provide benefits for the seller's family in perpetuity.

The flexibility of the EOT also comes into play with how the business distributes its profits to employee-owners. A selling owner has a great deal of leeway in setting up the guidelines for how a profit-sharing program operates. However, to comply with international ethical standards and to be considered a majority employee-owned business, the business should distribute the majority of its surplus profits to all tenured employees based on a neutral formula.

Moreover, an EOT company may include an equity component for key employees or senior leaders using stock or synthetic equity, e.g., a phantom stock or stock appreciation rights plan. An owner can also defer on making decisions regarding how profits are distributed and leave it up to future boards of directors to determine. For example, a future board of directors might decide to leverage the additional cash surplus generated by the business to award a mix of cash bonuses and employer contributions to employee 401(k) plans. The flexibility of the EOT allows the trust to be structured in ways that can best reward a company's employees.

Consider the example of a boutique business services firm the author advised. As spelled out in its trust agreement, the firm reserves a portion of its annual profits for its CEO and another portion as a bonus for its lowest-paid employees. The trust also specifies that a certain amount of surplus profits must be allocated to cash reserves. Most of its profits are then shared with the whole team, with the added stipulation that longstanding employees who have been with the firm for 10 years or more receive twice the bonus amount that new employees receive. By contrast, another EOT company, a large manufacturing firm also advised by the author, keeps things simple by sharing a portion of its profits equally among full-time employees. These examples demonstrate how flexible the EOT can be in meeting the needs of entrepreneurs with personalized and detailed visions for the future of their businesses under employee ownership.

Another area where EOTs offer flexibility is in how the business is governed. A selling business owner may decide on any number of alternatives when it comes to laying out how and who gets appointed to the company's board of directors, whether such a board will include employee-owners, and, if so, how many. The flexibility of the EOT also offers the seller opportunities to maintain "effective control" of the business even after the transaction closes, e.g., by retaining the power to appoint the company's board of directors, which is discussed later in this chapter.

3. Lower Cost

EOTs can be created through a highly efficient and low-cost process. Additionally, year-after-year maintenance costs with an EOT can be zero, depending on how the trust's governance is structured. These low costs can be attractive to entrepreneurs who prefer that the surplus generated by the business be reinvested in the company or its people rather than being used to pay outside service providers.

4. Simplicity

One of the primary reasons business owners are attracted to EOTs is how simple they are to put in place. With the help of a skilled advisor, an EOT can be put in place in as little as two months. Perhaps just as important, the concept of sharing profits in the business with the people who work there is straightforward and easy to understand. This can be a real advantage in terms of engaging employee-owners, who immediately understand the benefit conferred to them through their company's EOT profit-sharing plan.

5. Sustainability

One of the least understood or perhaps overlooked potential downsides to ESOP companies is that they can be sold to a third party without employee or founder approval. When an ESOP company receives a legitimate offer that is at a substantial premium over the most recent appraisal, the board must pass the offer on to the trustee. The trustee, in turn, has to assess how employees would fare from the sale *as participants in a retirement plan, not as employees*. The company can pass the vote on this issue through to employees, but even then, the trustee could, in theory, override the employee vote (although this has never happened). In practice, ESOP companies are often sold when a buyer offers a really attractive price. That is what happened at New Belgium Brewing, which was a proud ESOP company for two decades. It included the "Employee-Owned" tag on its product label. New Belgium's employees were allowed to vote on any offer, and when they got a very attractive one from Kirin Brewing, they voted yes by a large margin. This possibility, even if limited, is enough to convince some business owners that an EOT, which can be structured as a perpetual trust, is a better choice. An EOT provides more assurance that whatever their vision for the business is can be retained for the long term.

At the same time, EOTs don't have to last forever. EOTs allow the selling owner to specify the precise conditions under which a sale of the business would be permitted and how the proceeds should be distributed, e.g., to the employee-owners or charity. It's also possible to combine an EOT with a family trust if it makes sense as a part of a business owner's estate-planning strategy.

In plain terms, with an EOT, a business owner can customize when, how, and under what terms they would want to allow for the company to be sold out from under employee ownership. This means that for any entrepreneur concerned about the long-term sustainability of the business they created, an EOT allows them to install the kinds of defenses that will guarantee that the company will remain employee-owned for the long haul.

Making The Best Deal Possible

A thoughtful and considerate approach to an EOT transaction should help sellers feel safe, comfortable, and protected. When business owners sell to an EOT, they are well-protected on both sides of the transaction: (1) as a seller to the business who is able to maximize financial returns and retain significant enforcement power over the seller note (i.e., the seller becomes "the bank") and (2) as a fiduciary of the EOT with the opportunity to retain effective control of the business even after the sale.

Maximizing Financial Returns

One of the provisions that was put into place to help encourage business owners to sell to an ESOP is known as the "1042 rollover." This refers to a provision in the Internal Revenue Code (Section 1042) that allows business owners to defer capital gains tax when selling their closely held C corporation stock to an ESOP. Under the 1042 rules, when a business is sold to an ESOP, the seller can defer the capital gains tax on the proceeds from the sale if certain conditions are met, such as reinvesting the proceeds from the stock sale in qualified replacement property (QRP) within a specific time frame. QRP includes stocks and bonds of U.S. companies.

As compelling as the 1042 rollover might seem on paper, the option isn't as helpful as it might seem at first glance. For example, there are many restrictions on where the proceeds from a sale can be invested—real estate is not an option, for example, including investing in real estate investment trusts (REITs). The stocks and bonds of international companies are also excluded. This limits how much a seller can truly diversify their investments. This is to say nothing about the costs of borrowing the cash required for purchasing QRP within a year of the sale to an ESOP.

It's also critical to recognize that section 1042 enables a deferral of capital gains taxes, not an exemption. A 1042 sale works best if the goal is to pass on the wealth generated from the sale of a business (i.e., the QRP) to the seller's heirs or if the shares are held for a significant period after the ESOP transaction. In the former situation, the QRP would pass tax-exempt to the heirs. But this benefit disappears, relative to an EOT, if the sale of a business to an EOT is deferred until after the death of the owner. Under quite ordinary estate tax rules, all property receives a step-up in basis at the time of death. This means that all property receives a capital gains tax exemption if sold after the time of death. This fact effectively erases the major tax difference between ESOPs and EOTs.

In short, depending on how long the assets are held and the tax rate of the state where the owner resides, the ESOP may not offer as much in the way of maximizing after-tax financial returns as it may seem for some owners. In contrast, an EOT involves far less red tape in the process of establishing the selling price of a business. In selling to an ESOP, a business owner must follow strict rules for determining the fair market value of the business. A major part of the process of selling to an ESOP involves negotiating the sale price with a third-party trustee. Failing to follow the letter of the law or failing to operate honestly and in good faith can leave the seller and trustee open to future legal scrutiny and, potentially, litigation.

However, in selling to EOTs, the rules are far simpler––the seller and their company agree internally on the fair market value of the business. Of course, it is advisable to obtain a third-party valuation, but this is not necessary. Also, as should be clear in this comparison, there is no negotiation with a third-party trustee. If the company has a single shareholder who also serves as the sole board director and CEO, there is no negotiation at all. Of course, ordinary IRS rules apply with respect to fair market value, and if a sale to an EOT is audited by the IRS, it is possible for ordinary penalties to be imposed if the sale price significantly varies from fair market value. However, these rules and penalties are not specific to EOTs––they apply to all sales of business interests. Nonetheless, the above considerations certainly warrant care in selecting an advisor for an EOT transaction.

The above should also help to mitigate some of the concerns that business owners might have when considering whether they are "leaving money on the table" by selling to an EOT when compared to what a private equity firm might have paid for the business. If a business owner receives a competitive offer from a private equity buyer, they can use that figure as an important data point in establishing the fair market value of the company for a sale to an EOT. However, the closing price on a sale to private equity rarely matches the initial offer. Private equity firms have gained some renown for whittling the price down during the due diligence process and over the course of negotiations. That often puts business owners in a bind when, after months or even years of negotiating, they are given a take-it-or-leave-it offer that falls short of what they were initially offered. Private equity offers are also often contingent on the seller's continued employment with the firm, as well as the company's achievement of certain metrics laid out in the sale agreement. If a business owner chooses to sell to an EOT, on the other hand, there are no such back-and-forth negotiations. And there is no "moving target" in arriving at the final sale price years after the actual date of the sale. With an EOT, the sale price is the sale price.

Effective Control

A primary concern many entrepreneurs have when they sell their business is how the business will fare once they leave. Selling to an EOT gives those owners the ability to assert effective control of the business even after the sale. The form and degree of this effective control depends on the design of the trust.

For example, one of the areas in which a seller can assert continued influence on the business is the appointment of the company's board of directors. It might be desirable, for instance, for the seller to have a seat on the board, at least until the seller's note is paid in full. By having influence over the board, the seller would then have authority to affect other levers of control within the company, such as who serves as CEO or what policies are enacted. Over time, after the seller note has been paid, the rules of how board members are appointed can change. The EOT could adopt the very same "circular governance" approach used at most ESOP companies, in which the board of directors is essentially self-appointing. Alternatively, and depending on the vision of the seller, the EOT might grant voting rights to employee-owners for one or more seats on the board.

Another area in which the seller might want to have influence over the company's operations——and one of the more challenging aspects of designing an EOT——is determining the rules for the profit-sharing program. A seller might be concerned that the program could harm the business by not reinvesting profits back into the business to ensure its continued growth and stability. However, the EOT can be designed to allow the seller to have effective control over the levels of reinvestment, the manner in which profits are distributed, and, crucially, the aggressiveness of the firm's repayment of the seller note, at least until the seller note is repaid. This type of decision-making power might be especially critical in capital-intensive industries like manufacturing and less of a concern in more service-heavy sectors.

As noted above, when an EOT is seller-financed, the former owner is put in the position of a benevolent banker who can adjust their expectations and demands to the market conditions that the business is weathering. This power allows the selling owner to help the firm by deferring payments and extending the loan term, thus ensuring the firm's sustainability and growth. By the same token, if the business is struggling to make good on its obligations to the seller, the seller does have the power to assert direct control over the business, just as any bank would.

With that said, the seller should appoint an independent fiduciary to help legitimize the EOT in the eyes of employee-owners and to help confer economic substance on the underlying transaction. But the mandate of the independent fiduciary will be to enforce the trust provisions put into place by the seller—not those legislated by Congress under ERISA. The only enforcement regime that applies is state trust law, where the overwhelming mandate is to enforce the intentions of the person who created the trust in the first place. In the case of an EOT, this means the selling owner.

The Future of Employee Ownership

Entrepreneurs have a bias for action—and results. That drive is what makes them successful. But that same drive can make it difficult to look ahead and envision a future for their business without them. The EOT provides a happy medium. An owner can sell their business while continuing to have a say in how the business goes forward, as well as who will be making the decisions that will determine the fate of their company and their employees, now and in future generations. And they can accomplish this through a simpler path to employee ownership that maximizes their financial returns. That's a win-win.

CHAPTER 3

Setting Up the Trust

Steve Virgil

OW EMPLOYEE OWNERSHIP TRUSTS (EOTs) are legally organized seems to generate a good deal of confusion. This short chapter hopes to clarify at least some of this by placing the legal structure of an EOT within existing trust law and providing a way to navigate what may be a confusing topic. While an area of relatively new interest in the U.S., as far as legal structure is concerned, the EOT is organized and operates in ways that are very similar to other, more familiar, trusts. It may be useful to describe a little about trusts separately from EOTs to illustrate better how the EOT fits within this framework.

Trusts are separate legal entities that can hold property, manage assets, and make decisions. Like all legal entities, such as corporations and limited liability companies, agents for trusts do these things. At a basic level, a trust may be seen as a container of sorts, which is managed by another person and holds assets. This basic relationship involves three parties: the party who transfers assets into trust (the trustor), the party who receives the benefit of those assets after they are transferred (the beneficiary), and the party who is responsible for managing the use of those assets for their intended purpose (the trustee). The assets, once transferred, are called the "corpus" or "principal." The rules for how the assets may be used and the responsibilities placed on the trustee are described in detail in a document known by various names—the "trust agreement," "trust indenture," or simply the "trust."

As a separate legal entity, a trust is governed and operates independently from the trustor, trustee, and beneficiary. A trust may hold nearly all types of property and engage in almost all kinds of activities or business. State law will define in detail what a trust may or may not do, but for the purposes of EOTs, it is almost certainly the case that a trust may own and hold shares of stock or a membership interest in a limited liability company. This facet of the trust structure thus enables the EOT to be created.

Once formed, the EOT has three parts: (1) the corpus, consisting of the business that is transitioning to employee ownership, which may take the form of either shares in the business or the assets of the business; (2) the beneficiary, meaning the group of employees who benefit by receiving enhanced profit sharing or some similar benefit; and (3) the trustee, an individual or company that agrees to serve in the role of managing the trust to ensure it serves its purpose. Many EOTs also establish a "trust protector," a person who serves to ensure the intent of the trust is preserved over time. These elements are discussed below.

Structuring the EOT

1. *Trust formation:* The first step in establishing an EOT is to create a trust. This is typically done by the company's existing owners or shareholders and involves drafting the trust agreement. The trust agreement will contain significant detail about how the trustee will own the shares and to what use trust income, if any, will be put. The trust is a legal entity that holds the shares of the company on behalf of the employees.

2. *Trustees:* A trustee is then appointed, and this person or company will be responsible for overseeing the trust's operation and ensuring that the trust acts in the best interests of the employees. Trustees can be independent professionals, existing company management, or a combination of both.

3. *Ownership transfer:* The company's existing owners or shareholders sell or gift their shares to the EOT. The trust then holds these shares on behalf of the employees. The purchase of shares is typi-

cally funded through various mechanisms, such as loans from a third party or through contributions from the company in an earnout process. Note that the transfer usually involves financing and requires the typical documents and security involved in such a transaction. Business owners hoping to establish an EOT should be mindful that S corporation shares may be held in trust only under limited circumstances and that a conversion to C status may be needed to effectuate the transfer in a tax-efficient way.

4. *Employee benefits:* Because the trust owns the company shares, the employees become indirect beneficiaries of the trust. This means they are entitled to certain benefits, such as dividends or increases in share value, depending on the company's performance.

5. *Governance structure*: EOTs usually employ a unique governance structure, one that is slightly different from both more common trusts and closely held corporations. In this structure, the company is governed by a board that is responsible for management. Most often, that board includes employee representation. While independent of the company, employees usually have ways to inform the trustee about significant issues, either through a standing workers' committee or on specific issues as they arise, such as a decision to sell the company.

Structuring the EOT will require preparing various legal documents, including the trust agreement, share purchase agreements, the security agreement, governance documents such as bylaws, and employee benefit mechanisms. Together, these documents outline the rights and responsibilities of the trust, the trustees, and the employees.

Types of Trusts and the EOT

There are several different types of trust. For purposes of the EOT, only two are usually relevant: the grantor trust and the perpetual trust. Which trust is better suited to a particular business transfer depends on specific details of state law as well as the goals of the parties when establishing the trust relationship.

The Grantor Trust

Business owners may use a grantor trust to establish and make contributions in the name of employee beneficiaries to create a source of funding for the EOT transfer. The grantor trust is often useful when the business owner is financing the transition to the EOT. However, federal tax law conditions the beneficial tax treatment of a grantor trust on the requirement that the trust fund remains subject to the claims of the employer's creditors as if the assets were the general assets of the employer. Trustees are bound to act in the highest good faith toward their beneficiaries. This means that fiduciaries must discharge their duties solely in the interest of, and for the exclusive purposes of providing benefits to, participants and their beneficiaries, minimizing employer contributions thereto, and defraying reasonable expenses of administering the system.

A grantor trust is a trust arrangement in which the grantor, the individual who creates the trust and contributes assets to it, retains a certain amount of control over the trust and its assets for tax purposes. In a grantor trust, the grantor is typically responsible for paying income tax on the income generated by the trust, even though the trust itself technically owns the assets.

In a grantor trust, the grantor retains control over certain aspects of the trust, such as the ability to revoke or amend the trust, direct investments, or receive income from the trust assets. This control is what distinguishes a grantor trust from other types of trusts.

For tax purposes, the IRS treats the grantor as the owner of the trust assets, meaning that the grantor is responsible for reporting the income generated by the trust on their personal tax return. This allows the grantor to take advantage of certain tax benefits and deductions associated with the trust assets.

Grantor trusts can be either revocable or irrevocable. In a revocable grantor trust, the grantor retains the ability to revoke or amend the trust at any time. In an irrevocable grantor trust, the grantor typically relinquishes this ability but still maintains a certain amount of control over the trust for tax purposes.

Grantor trusts can be complex legal arrangements with significant tax implications, so it is important for individuals considering this type of trust to consult with legal and tax professionals to ensure that it aligns with their goals and objectives.

With a grantor trust, the trust corpus technically remains the property of the employer until the assets are distributed to the beneficiaries when any financing debt is satisfied. This structure provides tax advantages, as the employee beneficiaries are not taxed on their portion of the trust corpus or proceeds until distribution. However, the trust fund remains subject to the claims of the employer's creditors as if the assets were the employer's general assets.

The Perpetual Trust

A perpetual trust, also known as a perpetual or dynasty trust, is a type of trust designed to exist indefinitely, potentially lasting for multiple generations. Unlike many other types of trusts that have a predetermined termination date or event, a perpetual trust is structured to continue for as long as legally permissible. Perpetual trusts have no set expiration date, allowing them to endure for many generations, potentially indefinitely. The trust document may specify that the trust will continue until a certain event occurs, such as the termination of the trust by a court order or the depletion of trust assets.

One of the primary purposes of a perpetual trust is to provide ongoing asset protection for beneficiaries. By keeping assets within the trust structure, they can be shielded from potential creditors, lawsuits, divorces, or other claims that may arise over time.

The choice of trustee is crucial in a perpetual trust, as the trustee will be responsible for managing trust assets and making distributions to beneficiaries over the long term. Families may choose a corporate trustee, such as a bank or trust company, or appoint a trusted family member or advisor to serve as trustee.

In most states, perpetual trusts must provide a mechanism for the trustee to sell the trust assets. The trust document can include provisions for changing circumstances, allowing trustees to adapt to new challenges and opportunities. This almost certainly means that the trust agreement must provide for employee decisions or approval around decisions to sell or transfer trust property.

The establishment and administration of perpetual trusts are subject to specific legal requirements, which vary depending on jurisdiction. While most states no longer limit the duration of a trust, some states do have a law that limits the duration of trusts, known as the Rule Against Perpetuities. It is vitally important to work with an experienced attorney in the state where the trust will be established to navigate these rules.

The Trustee, Trust Protector, and Fiduciary Duties

Trustees of an EOT have a fiduciary duty to act in the highest good faith toward their beneficiaries and may not obtain any advantage over the beneficiaries by misrepresentation, concealment, threat, or adverse pressure of any kind. Fiduciaries must discharge their duties solely in the interest of, and for the exclusive purposes of providing benefits to, participants and their beneficiaries, minimizing employer contributions thereto, and defraying reasonable expenses of administering the system. A trust protector serves various powers and duties in the EOT structure, including the power to remove and replace trustees, veto or direct investments, change situs, terminate the trust, resolve conflicts among co-trustees or trustees and beneficiaries, and amend or reform the trust in light of changes in circumstances or law. A trust protector may also assume fiduciary duties, which could expose them to liability. Despite the significant role of trust protectors in many EOTs, few states have specific statutes addressing the trust protector's powers and duties.

The trust protector's role is most often one of assuring that the trustor's wishes and intent are preserved over time and may include a range of powers and duties that can be tailored to the specific needs of the trust and can include the ability to make significant decisions regarding the trust's administration. A trust protector may also assume fiduciary duties, which require them to act in the best interest of the trust and its beneficiaries. Failure to fulfill these duties could expose the trust protector to legal liability. The concept of a trust protector developed in the area of foreign trusts and offshore asset protection trusts and has been adopted domestically for various purposes, including the EOT. However, the lack of a specific statute in most states means that the role and duties of a trust protector may be largely defined by the terms of the trust itself.

CHAPTER 4

EOT Financing

Stacey Smith, Courtney Kemp, and Alison Lingane

𝒯RANSITIONING EXISTING BUSINESSES to employee ownership trusts (EOTs) through leveraged buyouts can significantly grow the employee ownership sector in the United States, especially by tapping the baby boomer retirement wave, or "silver tsunami."[1] Seller financing may fit the bill in many cases, and this is a common way of financing an EOT transition. In the coming years, as the pipeline of EOT deals grows beyond those business owners who are most inclined to employee ownership, the ability to provide upfront cash for a meaningful percentage of the transaction value, similar to traditional leveraged buyouts, will be critical. A range of capital sources is needed, and available capital to fund these deals will also need to grow. This chapter describes the different paths to financing an EOT sale, including outside capital (e.g., CDFI [Community Development Finance Institution] or bank financing), seller financing, and some hybrid models.

EOT Financing Overview

As an important form of broad-based employee ownership, an EOT can qualify for traditional employee ownership financing similar to fi-

---

1. See "Small Business Closure Crisis," https://project-equity.org/impact/small-business-closure-crisis/.

nancing tapped by employee stock ownership plans (ESOPs) or worker cooperatives. As long as the characteristics of the EOT include conveying some governance functions and financial benefit to the employees, lenders with experience lending to worker cooperatives or ESOPs— CDFIs, impact lenders, and some banks—will look to provide debt to finance the sale to the EOT.

Once an EOT has been designed and a deal has been finalized, the new employee-owned business takes on the loan or loans to purchase the company from the selling owner. These loans are paid off over time from the future operating profits of the company. The selling owner receives an upfront payment for any portion of the sale price financed by the outside lenders, and they receive payments over time for the remainder of the sale price financed by the seller.

Exact requirements vary from lender to lender, but a hallmark of employee ownership financing is that personal guarantees may not be required of employees or selling owners for employee ownership transition loans. Interest rates also tend to be favorable when financing comes from CDFIs or impact-focused loan funds. For example, during the period of higher interest rates in 2023, of the CDFIs that finance employee ownership on an ongoing basis, interest rates did not move with Fed rate increases. Some states have guarantee programs to help underwrite risk. State and federal policy changes are also in play to incentivize employee ownership. These include making financing more accessible and broadening tax benefits to selling owners. The Small Business Administration (SBA) recently updated its guidelines for its 7a loan guarantee program to help ESOPs access transition loans, but it will require federal legislation to remove the personal guarantee requirement for all SBA-backed loans for employee ownership transition financing.

Types of EOT Financing

Many of the EOTs we see today in the U.S. have been completely seller-financed, which achieves a quick transaction and one that is fully customizable to the selling owner's preferences, though requiring a longer time to repay and often some involvement from the selling owner over that period. Some selling owners prefer to explore outside senior debt alongside seller financing so they can receive a larger payout at the time of the sale. For EOTs to be a good alternative for business owners who are not specifically attracted to employee ownership, we need to avoid relying on 100% seller financing. A comprehensive look at EOT financing options includes the following instruments:

1. Senior debt from banks, CDFIs, employee ownership loan funds, or other impact lenders

2. Junior and subordinate debt from the selling owner(s)

3. Voting and non-voting preferred equity, and mezzanine debt

Senior debt takes the form of a term loan from one or more lenders. Lenders fall into different categories: commercial banks, CDFIs, or specialized employee ownership funds (many of which leverage impact investments). Most institutions will finance up to an amount based on a multiple of EBITDA (e.g., 2.5x) or a debt repayment ratio of somewhere around 1.20–1.25 (inclusive of all debt). Most loan terms are three to six years, although there can be exceptions depending on a company's situation. A senior lender typically needs to see part of the sale price financed by the selling owner(s) in the form of a subordinated seller note, so the senior lender might lend 40% to 70% of the overall sale price. While there are no known instances of an outside lender financing 100% of the sale price, we do see scenarios in which up to 80% of the price is financed through senior debt, depending on unique risk factors and company performance. Interest rates on senior debt vary based on the market and the underlying source of funds.

There are important drivers for senior debt financing from the perspective of the seller, the business, and the broader field of employee ownership. For the selling owner, outside financing means they can receive some cash at the time of sale, which is often important for personal reasons. For more mainstream business owners (who might not be attracted to employee ownership if they must use 100% seller financing), outside financing can make employee ownership possible, which broadens employee ownership's growth potential. For the business, senior debt means that it (in its new ownership form) is beginning its journey to establishing a credit history, which can be crucial to future growth and obtaining credit products when necessary. Lender underwriting is also an important check on the feasibility of a deal structure, ensuring that the deal is not putting undue pressure or leverage on the business. Going through the loan application and underwriting process is also an important capacity-building exercise for future leaders of the employee-owned business. Finally, for the employee ownership field, increasing the number of lenders and investors bringing capital to the space increases the momentum for additional deals and removes the capital access barrier.

Junior, or subordinate, debt carries an interest rate higher than senior debt. Seller notes are also junior and usually take the form of a promissory note or an earnout (or sometimes both). This debt will comprise the difference between the senior debt and the total sale price and typically amounts from 30% to 60% of the overall sale price. The term of this debt can be anywhere from 5 to 10 years, and in some cases longer if necessary to support the deal structure. It also typically extends beyond the term of the senior debt (it cannot be shorter). Interest rates vary and are usually a few to several points above senior debt. Other sources of financing are also possible to finance an EOT transition, including non-voting preferred equity and mezzanine debt.

Partial Sales

If the EOT owns less than 100% of the company stock, the remaining portion of the business can be financed by the full range of small business financing (including voting equity). Indeed, EOTs are a very effective vehicle for partial sales, in which only a percentage of equity is transferred to the trust, and the selling owner retains a percentage of equity. In the case of a partial sale or even a progressive sale, the selling owner can begin by placing 30%–49% of equity into the trust to gain liquidity and diversify their assets. Then, when they are ready to exit completely, they can sell the remaining equity. They could begin with a smaller percentage if desired, although 30% is the minimum threshold for becoming certified as employee-owned through Certified EO. During the period of paying off a partial sale, the company can raise additional capital using non-voting equity, if desired. That can be an important consideration for business owners if their goal is to continue to grow the business, ensuring broad-based employee ownership is not a constraint to using traditional investment methodologies.

Vision for Transaction Financing

Exploring transaction financing objectives, desired outcomes, and motivations early in the process with the selling owner and key employees can yield a good roadmap for how to proceed with financing. Through early conversations, the deal team—selling owner and key employee representatives—can hone in on the financing mix most appropriate for the deal. Based on their financial and tax situations, selling owners have specific capacity and timing issues that must be understood and accounted for in the final mix of capital. There may also be other considerations, including the credit product needs of the business after transitioning to EOT ownership and assessing whether the senior debt provider can fill these needs.

Senior Debt Considerations

Lender Identification

There are multiple ways to identify potential capital providers. Developing a financing request for proposal (RFP) or request for a letter of interest (LOI) can be a great way to solicit interested providers. Documents such as these should include details about the business—industry, history, organizational structure, management, and historical financial performance—as well as details on the key employee ownership design decisions affecting control and benefit for employee-owners. They should also include information about the proposed deal structure. This typically includes the sale price, proposed sources of funds (including subordination), use of funds, and transaction timing. Working with a technical assistance provider with some experience in sourcing capital for EOT transitions can help expand the list of capital providers to solicit.

Evidence of Employee Control and Benefit

For CDFI or impact lenders that are aligned with employee ownership to offer transaction financing to an EOT, there will need to be evidence of employee-owner control and benefit. The easiest way to convey this information is to summarize the governance role for employees as well as the financial benefit options tied to ownership. These are typically found in the trust agreement, corporate bylaws, or other policy documents. At a minimum, most capital providers want to see pass-through voting on significant issues, representation for employees on governing bodies, and provisions for profit sharing tied to ownership for employees. There may be other details related to governance and/or financial benefits tied to ownership for employees that can also be shared with potential lenders. Capital providers may also consider the percent of equity placed in the trust, with a minimum threshold for some lenders of 30%.

Loan Application and Underwriting

Each capital provider will have a unique application packet and process to be followed. It is important to communicate with lenders early in the transition process, allowing the deal team to fully understand the application process and prepare for a successful application. Typical information to be submitted will include basic business information, such as legal structure and a list of applicable certifications; management information, such as an organizational chart and key leadership bios; financial data, such as historical financial performance and projected financial performance; and information on the new employee-owned business structure, including leadership and governance details. In many cases, lenders will want to review the foundational legal documents for the employee-owned business, including the trust agreement and corporate bylaws, and in some cases, they will want to know about the demographics of company employees. In all cases, applicants can expect one to three due diligence calls with lenders as they learn more about the company and its future employee ownership plans.

Although the involvement of an outside lender creates additional requirements compared to a 100% seller-financed transaction, the application process is on par with, and perhaps even less burdensome than, traditional requirements. Employee ownership lenders can be more flexible than traditional lenders in some cases. At times, for example, preliminary financial information and draft governing documents can be submitted at the application point and final information conveyed when available. Additionally, the lenders most suited to assisting EOT clients through applications to finance employee ownership transitions are also more mission-oriented than traditional lenders. They are extremely motivated to support the success of the transition, and they tend to serve as valuable resources for companies transitioning to employee ownership through the application process and beyond.

Security and Guarantees

If the business has meaningful assets, the senior lender may securitize the loan by taking an interest in business assets that are pledged as collateral. However, many small businesses do not have collateral anywhere near the value of the loan. As a result, most EOT loans are cash flow loans, paid back out of the future profits of the business. In some cases, employee ownership lenders that specialize in cash flow loans may look for creative ways to bring in some security, for example, requiring a life insurance policy for the top leader to be pledged.

In small business lending, SBA loan guarantees frequently play an important role. However, as of this writing, the SBA still requires a personal guarantee for EOT loans, which is typically not an approach that makes sense for a business with broad-based employee ownership. Which one of the 20, 75, or 500 employee-owners should be personally responsible for the loan? Some states offer loan guarantee programs that may be a fit for employee ownership. For example, the California Infrastructure Bank (IBank) can guarantee up to 80% of the value of the loan amount. Project Equity has successfully tapped the IBank Loan guarantee program for California transitions of other forms of broad-based employee ownership and expects that it would be possible to tap the guarantee for EOTs.

Seller/Junior Debt Considerations

Seller Requirements

It is important to surface and understand the seller's goals, preferences, and capacity for providing a portion of financing early in the transition. Identifying the selling owner's goals will point to how best to structure the seller portion of the capital stack. Considerations include whether the seller needs cash at the time of closing to fund any personal commitments and how much they require; personal factors such as seller age, health, and other personal characteristics; and how comfortable they are in offering seller financing to the future business. The answers to these questions will inform the bank/seller "split" of the overall sale price (alongside the lender's perspective on the split). It is also important to understand how the seller prefers to receive payments over time, their appetite for risk, and how satisfied they are with the sale price. The answers to these questions will inform the details of the seller financing (split, term, rate, etc.).

Debt Form (Note and/or Earnout)

The most common type of seller financing is a seller note. This note will be between the seller and the business, with payments generally received by the selling owner every month. Loan sizes and payback periods are fixed when using a seller note. The business will repay the note out of operating cash flows based on the terms of the note, and interest rates are set at an appropriate rate commensurate with the risk and applicable federal rates (AFR). Typically, the terms of the seller note will allow for loan restructuring in the event of financial hardship of the business.

Another common type of seller financing is an earnout—a performance-based payout. Like seller notes, earnouts are agreements between the seller and the business, but the owner generally receives payments annually rather than monthly. Seller proceeds are not fixed when using an earnout, although the payback period will be fixed for a certain number of years. Earnouts are flexible instruments. Generally, they are calculated on an annual basis and written as a percentage of either net income or total revenue. They can be supplemental to a seller note, or they can be the sole form of seller financing, depending on the preferences of the selling owner and the flexibility of the senior lender(s). Earnouts may also include a "floor," or minimum annual payment the selling owner can expect, or a "ceiling," or maximum annual payment the business would be required to pay the selling owner. Because seller proceeds are determined based on business performance, they are creative and useful tools for parties to come to an agreement, allowing the selling owner the opportunity for additional upside if the business performs well and protecting the future business in years of downturn.

Security and Intercreditor Agreement

The seller does not take any specific security in exchange for the note or an earnout. Instead, the note or earnout will be specifically subordinate to any senior debt. As a result, seller financing commonly features term lengths 6–12 months longer than senior debt terms. Any seller financing will also include an intercreditor agreement between the seller holding the debt and the senior note holder. It can be the case that a senior debt holder will not allow principal repayment on a seller note before the senior note is fully paid off, though we have not seen that with an EOT transaction.

Case Studies

The two case studies below illustrate two different approaches to financing a transition to an EOT. One, a medium-sized retail business, used a mix of senior debt between participating lenders plus seller financing in the form of a loan. Another, a small manufacturing business, used 100% seller financing via a progressive sale plus a cash flow waterfall repayment strategy.

Case Study 1: Medium-Sized Retail Business

This longstanding business was a consistently profitable, debt-free, and growing brand. The company's values had been the focal point of all operations since inception, and all 75 employees strove to maintain environmental, social, and economic sustainability as part of their business practices. As they began to analyze succession options, the selling owner wanted to lock in a model that would protect the long-term financial and organizational sustainability of the company, give employees the opportunity to benefit from the company's success, and preserve the legacy and culture of the company in the long term. They evaluated ownership succession options that would enable them to exit and pass ownership to their staff, and in 2022, made the decision to transition 100% of their stock into an EOT.

Preserving the mission and values of the company—as well as ensuring that current and future employees had the opportunity to engage in governance and to benefit from and share in the profits of the business—was of key importance to the selling owner. At the same time, the selling owner preferred to have a liquidity event at the time of sale. With the help of a technical assistance provider, the selling owner issued an RFP to identify a mission-aligned lender that could provide the company with a fixed-rate term loan at the lowest overall borrowing cost to finance the mission-aligned buyout of the company by the EOT. The RFP included loan size details, a description of the seller financing to be offered to the business in conjunction with the senior debt, and other key business information that might usually be contained in a business plan (e.g., information on business performance, history, strategy, and management). The RFP requested that interested lenders respond with draft pricing, terms, and an initial due diligence request list.

Ultimately, Shared Capital Cooperative led the financing round for this business. The loan was provided as part of Accelerate Employee Ownership, a joint initiative of Shared Capital and Project Equity, with Project Equity's Employee Ownership Catalyst Fund participating for a portion of the transaction. The note was offered at the requested total loan size listed in the RFP, with a term length of 84 months and an interest rate of 5.5%. Collateral included assets on hand, although these were limited compared to some other companies, and the company's future cash flows also secured the loan. A security agreement was drafted as part of the financing. Certain conditions were required as part of the loan agreement, including that the business maintain its status as an EOT-owned or other employee-owned business operating on a cooperative basis, as well as that it agree to provide impact data regarding job quality, employee demographics, and business performance to Project Equity in the form of a survey for the duration of the financing.

Shared Capital required that the selling owner carry a portion of the sale price. The selling owner offered a note to the business for about 40% of the overall sale price, which was subordinate to the note from Shared Capital but featured similar terms. An intercreditor agreement between the selling owner and the lead lender outlined the specifics of this agreement.

Case Study 2: Small Manufacturing Business

This business was a high-margin manufacturing company that had become extremely successful in its region. The company was already employee-focused before it transitioned to EOT ownership, and it had built a wonderful reputation for being a great place to work for its 35 employees. When the selling owner began to pursue exit options, they considered multiple types of employee ownership. Ultimately, in 2021, after evaluating the options available to them, they made the decision to transition the company to EOT ownership using a waterfall repayment strategy that provided the selling owner with a return while enabling the business to continue operating for the benefit of the current and future employees. The company stock was owned by the selling owner and a number of current and former employees. At the time of trust formation, the selling owner transferred their shares to the trust, and the company repurchased all outstanding shares held by employees, so the EOT became the 100% owner of the company.

This deal did not use senior debt, but it is a useful case study in revenue-based financing (RBF) and demonstrates an innovative solution to the need for financing choices. At the time of the purchase, all small shareholders were paid out completely, and the larger shareholders received a partial payment as well as proceeds from a 10-year seller note over time. This note was not for a fixed price but rather for an amount defined as a portion of the company's earnings each year. This structure enabled the company to pay more in profitable years and pay less in challenging years. These instruments commonly feature minimum or maximum payments, as desired by the seller or buyer, and they can be wonderful solutions to protect employee-owned businesses in the case of a downturn while allowing selling owners the opportunity for additional upside in the case of growth or high performance. In this case, a minimum annual payout was structured, and 10% of the note debt was to be retired annually regardless of the payout to the selling owner in that year. The company plans to finance this repurchase through its cash flows, using funds that would have gone to shareholder dividends had the sale not taken place. After 100% of the note is paid, these funds will provide profit-sharing rewards for employees.

Conclusion

Expanding the financing of EOTs beyond seller financing is important to grow the field of employee ownership, as it makes EOTs an increasingly viable option for business owners looking for a succession strategy. Combining a senior loan with subordinated seller financing offers the most flexibility for the selling owner and has been widely used for other forms of broad-based employee ownership.

To best meet the needs of each business, it is important to assess financing needs during the initial feasibility study to chart the best potential strategy. Understanding the business' debt capacity looking forward is critical to establishing the financing approach. Working closely with the seller to assess their financing capacity, interest, and limitations is also important, as the combination of what the business can take on and what the seller is interested in (or willing to) finance creates the guardrails for structuring the deal.

Identifying lenders early in the process will also save everyone headaches, as outside lenders can be brought along as the contours of the deal come into focus. Identifying the lender(s) early helps the business prepare for its underwriting requirements. Technical assistance providers with experience in EOTs are likely to know lenders that are open to financing EOT transactions. The good news is that the stable of lenders that are open to financing EOTs is growing as more business owners turn to this form for their employee ownership transitions.

EOTs are a very valuable form of broad-based employee ownership, given the flexibility of their structure. Expanding financing will, in turn, help expand the growth of EOTs in the U.S.

CHAPTER 5

Governance and Ownership Culture in EOTs

*Anne-Claire Broughton and
Courtney Kemp*

$\mathcal{A}$S DESCRIBED IN THIS BOOK, employee ownership trusts (EOTs) can be a good fit for lower middle-market and smaller firms (those with revenues up to $50 million) and those that want to share profits with employees but prefer flexibility in governance and overall design versus the regulations of an ESOP or worker cooperative. This chapter explores the emerging field of EOTs, focusing on governance and culture and using case studies of two very different EOTs to illustrate key principles.

What Is an EOT?

Broad-based employee ownership refers to the ownership of a company, in part or in whole, by some or all of its employees. People have different views about what ownership entails. One key tenet of broad-based employee ownership can be *control* (the ability of employees to meaningfully participate in company governance and shape their experience in the workplace); a second is *benefit* (the provision of wealth-building possibilities in the form of higher-than-market-rate compensation, profit sharing related to ownership, retirement savings accounts, health insurance, and/or financial education and counseling, for instance). Actual equity ownership is often seen as an essential part of what it means to be an employee-owner, but as this book discusses, EOT proponents argue that the other elements described in this paragraph are sufficient.

Although EOTs are a relatively nascent strategy for achieving broad-based employee ownership in the U.S, they represent a promising model for inviting employees into the risks and rewards of small business ownership, and they serve as a viable third option for achieving meaningful broad-based employee ownership alongside ESOPs and worker coops. Unlike an ESOP or a worker coop, an EOT is a form of broad-based employee ownership for a business that typically uses the perpetual purpose trust (PPT) structure. Trusts are often used to protect the ownership of assets for the benefit of an individual or group of individuals (often family members). A trustee is named to safeguard these interests. Unlike a traditional trust, in which a person or persons is defined as the beneficiary of its assets, an EOT is established for the benefit of a *purpose:* employee ownership. An EOT is also unique in that, in many states, it is able to run in perpetuity instead of being limited to 21 years or the life of the grantor. A PPT is, therefore, a trust formed to protect the mission and operations of the company in perpetuity. After a PPT is formed, the selling owner sells or transfers their interest in the company to the trust, either all at once or in installments over time, often financing the transaction via a mix of bank financing and seller financing held by the company. The management and employees operate the company, and the trust holds and owns the company shares. Similarly to the ESOP and worker coop model, employees do not contribute to purchasing an ownership stake in the company, meaning that no upfront investment by employees is necessary.

EOTs are PPTs that are designed to confer certain elements of control and benefit to the company's employees. In an EOT, the trust's purpose is explicitly defined as the benefit of the employees. The EOT model is inherently flexible, and it can be designed to function more like an ESOP or more like a worker coop to suit the company's team, strategy, and culture. In terms of benefit, EOTs encourage wealth building via profit-sharing plans in which employees receive a percentage of ongoing profits, in accordance with a formula, throughout the duration of their employment. If desired, these profits can be channeled into a diversified 401(k) for retirement purposes, specifically enabling employees to build wealth over time. Other employee benefits may also be offered to employees at EOT companies, just as they might be for any worker coop or ESOP company. Additionally, EOTs provide the possibility of meaningful control of the company via employee participation and decision-making influence in corporate and trust governance; employee participation in meetings, training, and other types of education related to the company and employee ownership; and voting on certain key issues as designated by each company.

EOT Governance at a High Level

A business considering the use of a perpetual purpose trust should examine the state law it seeks to use before establishing the trust, as it may inform which governing structure will be required. If the state law limits the use of purpose trusts in the business context, the business can create the trust in another state. Oregon and Delaware are currently the only states that permit a purpose trust to last in perpetuity and do not give the court authority to reduce the amount in the trust. It may be best, therefore, for businesses to set up their trusts in one of those two states. Several other states permit a purpose trust to last in perpetuity but include a provision allowing a court to reduce the amount in the trust. Maine, Nevada, New Hampshire, South Dakota, and Wyoming all take this approach.

Generally, an EOT set up via a PPT has three key players in its governance ecosystem: a trust stewardship committee (TSC), a corporate board, and a trust protector (also known as a trust enforcer). All stakeholders share the common purpose of operating for the benefit of the current and future employees of the business. These three stakeholders can be thought of as the "three-legged stool" of governance in an EOT.

The *trust stewardship committee (TSC)* is responsible for overseeing the trust in accordance with the terms defined in the trust agreement, the document by which a PPT is to be governed. TSC members have a fiduciary duty to put the trust agreement and its stated purpose first in all decisions, and they hold and can exercise the full power to manage the trust property in accordance with the purposes outlined in the trust agreement. This means that TSC members are legally responsible and liable for executing the purpose of the trust.

The company must also have a *board of directors* to oversee its strategy and performance. Both the corporation and the trust share the purpose of operating for the benefit of the current and future employees of the corporation, and the board interacts with the TSC as designated by the company. As in a traditionally owned corporation, the board is responsible for overseeing the company in accordance with the terms defined in its corporate bylaws. Board members have a fiduciary duty to enhance the prosperity and viability of the company.

In Oregon and Delaware, a *trust enforcer* (also known as a *trust protector*) is a required element of the trust structure. The trust enforcer enforces the trust agreement in all circumstances, putting the trust's purpose first in all decisions. Primarily, the trust enforcer provides an avenue for escalation, serving as an independent arbitrator for grievances brought by various stakeholders. In such situations, the trust enforcer would be responsible for deciding whether the terms of the trust agreement have been violated. In a worst-case scenario, trust enforcers are empowered to take legal or other actions to enforce the trust's purpose.

One final requirement of the PPT legal structure is the involvement of a *directed corporate trustee,* although specifics regarding the trustee vary depending on the state in which the trust is sited. Generally, EOT trustees act according to the TSC's direction, and they have little to no decision-making authority within the EOT governance ecosystem. Because the trust directs them, the EOT trustee's powers and liability are significantly limited compared to the default powers of a typical trustee.

In practice, there is a wide scope of ways in which governance and employee participation can be structured, and there can be a blurring and blending of these structures to suit each company's needs. There is also flexibility in how the members of the various governing bodies are identified. It is important to remember that, for the most part, the nuances of how the trust works come down to decisions developed during the design phase of the new employee-owned company.

Additionally, the form in which decisions are made can be a mix of direct and representative democratic structures. Direct democracy includes members of an employee-owned company voting directly on key decisions of the business, while representative democracy includes employees voting for and electing members of the TSC or nominating candidates to the board to act on behalf of employees and the company. At most employee-owned companies, including EOT companies, representative rather than direct democracy is practiced.

Ownership Culture Development in an EOT

Like any employee-owned company, you can't just convert to employee ownership with an EOT and expect to have a fully fledged ownership culture where all employees are engaged and think like owners. It takes time and consistent education and coaching to help cultivate an ownership culture, regardless of the mode of employee ownership. Here are some important considerations when creating an employee ownership culture post-transition.

Include Diverse Employees at the Highest Level of Governance

For an EOT company to achieve a real sense of ownership among all team members, employees should be able to participate in governance, hold power, and represent their peers via governance. Even if an employee is not actively sitting on a governing body or serving in an official capacity, companies can encourage ownership culture and employee participation by consistently publishing meeting minutes, creating subcommittees that collect employee feedback, and setting up procedures that allow employees to contribute to the appointment and election of their peers to the various governing bodies.

Focusing on the diversity of employees representing their peers is also important. Diversity can mean different things in different companies. At an EOT company, it can mean representing a diversity of departments, roles, and positions in governance. For example, encouraging nonmanagement employees to serve as board directors and

TSC members can build trust between management and nonmanagement employees. It also serves as a powerful expression of employee ownership, signaling that the company considers employee opinions, values, and voices when making important decisions.

Maintain a Regular Communication Cadence at the Governance Level and with Employees

Corporate boards and TSCs generally meet quarterly, although the cadence can shift depending on company needs. All governance stakeholders are responsible for ensuring they are appropriately informed of each other's activity and keep up with the company's key health metrics via relevant reporting. This might consist of a periodic meeting of the board and TSC chairs to streamline communication and drive collaboration, the consistent sharing and review of meeting minutes, or other strategies. Similarly, the trust enforcer should attend regular and special TSC meetings as needed and review TSC minutes and other information related to TSC actions to stay appropriately informed.

Communicating with employees who are not members of the governing bodies is also a key piece of employee ownership engagement. An annual all-company meeting is a requirement of most employee-owned companies, and each company should also work toward transparency to employees on an ongoing basis throughout the year via open book management or a similar process (although the level of transparency is flexible based on what works best for each company). Consistent employee communication is key to increasing employee engagement.

Develop the Appropriate Tools to Maintain Clear Communication

Empowering employees to participate in governance yields positive benefits for companies, but it can be confusing for all parties involved if not managed appropriately. To increase clarity and reduce confusion, it is best practice for all employee-owned companies to draft and adopt a decision-making matrix outlining key decisions. These matrices generally include details about who is responsible for making the decision, who should be consulted and informed, how voting should occur, and anything else important to the company.

A key performance indicator (KPI) dashboard, or scorecard, related to company performance is another valuable tool that helps drive clarity among governing bodies. This tool can be referred to in governance meetings, and it may also include a dashboard related to the trust's purpose. Metrics for these dashboards vary from company to company but can include financial items such as net income and growth margins, profit sharing data such as the percentage of net income used for profit sharing or cumulative profit sharing, job quality information such as the percentage of staff with access to certain benefits or the turnover rate, and other information crucial to the performance, mission, and purpose of the company. These dashboards provide an important communication tool for boards, TSCs, and trust enforcers, and they drive accountability toward achieving the goals set forth in the corporate bylaws and trust agreement.

Be Prepared to Wear Multiple Hats

The "three-legged stool" of EOT governance can be burdensome if not approached with the right mindset. Although we have outlined the main EOT governing groups as distinct entities, many small businesses do not have enough employees to build governing bodies in which each person serves in only one role. For example, at some EOT companies, the CEO serves on the board, on the TSC, or as the trust enforcer. In others, one employee may serve on both the board and the TSC. All employees serving on a governing body will also continue their day-to-day operational work unrelated to governing tasks. In all of these cases, employees within the EOT will need to learn how to juggle multiple hats as part of the transition to employee ownership, switching between their operational and governance roles as required. It can take some practice to master this mindset shift, but over time, employees learn how to assess each topic through the lens of the hat they are wearing at that time. Ultimately, this can build the capacity of employees to address important issues as they arise and drive company performance over time.

Focus on Long-Term Knowledge and Capacity-Building of All Governance Stakeholders

At first, EOT knowledge and comprehension may be concentrated with a few key individuals. Over time, companies should work to disseminate information about the EOT among all employees in order to build the capacity of each person to participate. This can be done in a multitude of ways, including targeted training, PowerPoint presentations, and reading materials. A common tool to provide information to employees is an employee ownership handbook. Employee ownership handbooks generally contain detailed information about the EOT's purpose as well as information regarding policies and procedures related to the EOT. These could include nomination, appointment, and election procedures for the board and TSC; information around the financial benefit for employees, including when it is paid and how it is calculated; and information about the transition deal structure that is relevant to the employees, such as the term length on any debt.

This information must be accessible to all employees. Accessibility means that companies may need to translate materials into multiple languages and/or ensure they are written in a style every employee can absorb. If employees struggle with written communication, it may also mean prioritizing in-person meetings and verbal communication between managers and employees.

Another common practice is to have an employee committee focused on EOT education. Members of this committee are charged with understanding the EOT's purpose, structure, and governance and regularly communicating this to employees. This committee can help create and disseminate information from the employee ownership handbook and find ways to make the information accessible. Having a regular, consistent cadence of information and education is vital to making employee ownership real and tangible to employees at an EOT company.

With these best practices in mind, how EOT companies set up their governance and create or enhance an existing ownership culture varies greatly from company to company. Some are like one of the two examples below; others may have relatively limited employee involvement in governance. The data is compelling, however, that high-involvement cultures are strongly associated with company success. The two examples that follow show how to create this.

Case Studies

The case studies below on ShopBot Tools and Hummingbird Wholesale illustrate two different approaches to governance and creating an ownership culture at an EOT company. ShopBot Tools is based in North Carolina, which to date does not have Perpetual Purpose Trust legislation, whereas Hummingbird Wholesale is based in Oregon, which does have PPT legislation.

ShopBot Tools

Located in Durham, NC, ShopBot Tools is a manufacturer of computer numerical control (CNC) tools with 35 employees. These tools make it possible to do precision cutting of materials from computer designs and are used worldwide in diverse sectors, including manufacturing, cabinet and furniture making, sign making, education, and maker spaces. The business was founded in 1996 by Ted Hall, a professor of neuroscience at Duke University who wanted to build boats in his spare time and was looking for an affordable CNC tool to cut the parts efficiently. When he couldn't find even a used CNC router for less than $50,000, he built his own—and found an enthusiastic client base. The company grew from there.

By 2016, Ted had reached retirement age and was interested in exiting the business. At a conference he met Joseph Blasi, a leading employee ownership academic, and they had conversations about ESOPs as a potential exit vehicle. Employee ownership met Ted's goals of providing him with a financial return while enabling the business to continue operating for the benefit of current and future employees, ShopBot's dedicated worldwide community of customers, and the Durham, NC, community. However, after attending an NCEO conference and commissioning a basic feasibility study, Ted decided that an ESOP was not a good fit for ShopBot.

In early 2017, Ted was introduced to consultant Anne-Claire Broughton and engaged her to help the company implement the Great Game of Business's open-book management system. This served two purposes: it helped the company become more profitable, and it helped engage all the employees in understanding and tracking the key metrics of the business. Ted had always been very open with the financials, but open-book management was a deeper step into educating and engaging employees and became one of the foundations of ShopBot's ownership culture.

After open-book management was well established at ShopBot, Ted began exploring other forms of employee ownership. At another NCEO conference, he met Chris Michael, founder of EOT Advisors, learned more about EOTs, and ultimately decided to pursue one for ShopBot. An EOT allowed the company to essentially buy itself on behalf of the employees and remain employee-owned in perpetuity, continuing to serve the interests of the employees, customers, and the community.

With the help of Chris Michael, Anne-Claire Broughton, a local lawyer, and a local accounting firm, Ted and the ShopBot team closed on their EOT, the first in North Carolina, in June 2021. Ted chose to establish the trust in North Carolina rather than in a state such as Delaware with perpetual purpose trust legislation because that is where the company is based. He hoped this would encourage the state to develop PPT legislation and other support systems for EOTs.

The ShopBot EOT was 100% seller-financed. Ted owned 65% of the stock, and other key employees (current and former) owned the remaining 35%. At the trust's formation, Ted Hall transferred 100 shares of ShopBot stock to the trust, and then the company repurchased all outstanding shares held by individual shareholders so that the EOT now owned 100% of ShopBot. At purchase, the small shareholders were paid out completely, and the larger shareholders received partial payment and a 10-year note. An unusual feature of ShopBot's notes is that they are not for an absolute amount or a fixed valuation but rather an amount defined as a portion of ShopBot's earnings each year for 10 years. This enables the company to pay more in more profitable years and less in leaner years, although there is a minimum dollar amount that must be paid annually. Regardless of the exact dollar amount paid each year, 1/10th of the note debt is retired annually. Repurchases are largely covered by funds that would have gone to shareholder dividends, and these same funds will become the source for ownership reward bonuses for employees after the repurchase note has been paid.

Governance at ShopBot

ShopBot's EOT is guided by two documents, the ShopBot EOT Trust Agreement, which defines the terms of the trust, and the ShopBot EOT Terms of Governance, which lays out governance roles and responsibilities at the company. The four key players in ShopBot's governance structure are the board of directors, the trust protector, the trustee, and the Employee Governance Committee (EGC).

The ShopBot board of directors consists of outside directors, management, and employee representatives. The board is charged with setting strategic direction, selecting the CEO, reviewing company financials, and carrying out the ongoing profit sharing by the trust formulation. The trustee for ShopBot's EOT is an outside professional hired to ensure that the terms of the trust are being fulfilled. There is also a trust protector position, which is charged with appointing the trustee as well as designating alternate trustee candidates to replace the trustee should the trustee resign or be dismissed. Founder Ted Hall will serve as both trust protector and board chair until the turnover point (defined as either six years after the formation of the EOT, the date at which a certain amount of the total notes has been repaid, or the date at which all of the notes have been fully repaid). After the turnover point, the trust protector position will end, and the board chair will be elected by the board.

The CEO and other top company leaders (e.g., the COO and CFO) are charged by the board with the day-to-day operation of the business. Employees participate in overall governance through the EGC, for which all employees are eligible after one year of employment and completion of a training program in ShopBot history, structure, financial operations, and best practices in employee engagement. The ECG is charged with company-wide education about the EOT and open-book management, nominating and selecting employee representatives to the board of directors, and serving as an employee voice. The EGC meets at least once per quarter and usually two weeks before any board meetings. The EGC also convenes at least two all-employee meetings per year to garner employee feedback. The EGC consists of eight members who may serve multiple but nonconsecutive terms.

Creating an Ownership Culture at ShopBot

As mentioned above, the foundation of ShopBot's ownership culture is open-book management. Open-book management is an operating system designed to engage employees at every level to focus on the key metrics of the business. The goal is for everyone to think, feel, and act like an owner. It is more involved than simple transparency or sharing the income statement periodically. It helps improve the company's financial results and builds employee engagement at all levels. Weekly, all-company huddles provide a regular communication touchpoint for all aspects of the business as well as a conduit for employee ideas about how to improve the business. Finally, the bonus plan ensures that everyone knows the company's profitability goals and what they stand to gain by helping achieve those goals.

In addition to the weekly open-book management huddles, the main way that ShopBot builds its ownership culture is via its EOT educational training program, developed by consultant Anne-Claire Broughton and CEO Jeanne Taylor to help employees understand the EOT and how they can contribute to the company's success. The EOT training is designed to be accessible, meaningful, engaging, and interactive. It is delivered by members of the EGC, who helped design and vet the training, ensuring that it answered questions that employees would be likely to raise. The EOT training consists of three slide presentations with an accompanying script that the EGC members can adapt by illustrating stories from their own experiences: "1. What is the employee ownership trust?" "2. Why an EOT, and how does it work?" and "3. Who is responsible for running the company, and how are rewards distributed?" Each session is followed by a Kahoot? quiz to gauge the participants' retention of the information and encourage feedback, and the third session includes brainstorming on how employees can help the company succeed. This three-part training is delivered annually, along with an orientation to open-book management and financial literacy.

Hummingbird Wholesale

Located in Eugene, OR, Hummingbird Wholesale is a small-scale organic food manufacturer with 47 employees. The company acts as a force for good in local organic food systems, offering high-quality and nutritious foods grown locally and as sustainably as possible, partnering with local suppliers, and promoting environmental sustainability within the company and the local region.

Originally founded as a specialty honey shop in 1972, Hummingbird Wholesale was acquired by Charlie and Julie Tilt in 2003. After growing the company to what it is today, the Tilts began exploring employee ownership options to help them plan for succession while preserving the mission of the company. The Tilts wanted to lock in a model that would protect the long-term financial and organizational sustainability of the company, give employees the opportunity to benefit from the company's success, and preserve the legacy and culture of the company in the long term. In early 2022, Hummingbird Wholesale kicked off a feasibility assessment with Project Equity to assess the company's fit for employee ownership, deciding to undergo a transition process to employee ownership later that year. In early 2023, with the support of Project Equity and others, the selling owners placed 49% of the company's shares into a perpetual purpose trust sited in Oregon, and Hummingbird Wholesale transitioned to an EOT. A second sale for the remaining 51% of equity is locked in for 2028, ensuring that the business will become majority worker-owned and controlled.

Since Charlie and Julie Tilt took over the company, its mission has always been the focal point of all operations, and all coworkers strive to maintain environmental, social, and economic sustainability as part of their business practices. The EOT model locks in the values that the company has pursued over the last 20 years, and the trust agreement enshrines the most fundamental purposes of the trust: preserving the mission of the company, benefiting coworkers, maintaining the trust's ownership of the company in perpetuity, ensuring that the profits of the company are distributed primarily for the benefit of coworkers, and ensuring the long-term health of the company for the benefit of employees and the furtherance of the company mission.

Governance at Hummingbird

With the EOT came three new governance structures: a trust steward-ship committee (TSC), a corporate board, and a trust protector. To determine how these groups would be formed, Hummingbird Whole-sale created a working group of diverse coworkers during the design phase of the transition process. This group, called the transition team, took responsibility for certain governance design decisions, reviewed and contributed to the formation of the trust agreement and corporate bylaws, and communicated with and elicited feedback from the wider pool of coworkers. Charlie Tilt was a member of this team, and the par-ticipatory nature of the team built upon a culture already well-aligned with employee ownership in terms of transparency and participation. The ability for coworkers to participate in the design of the ownership and governance structure of the future company encouraged collabora-tion, and it demonstrated the commitment to involving the voices of more than just a few management figures. Perhaps most importantly, it increased the capacity of the transition team members to engage meaningfully with the employee ownership material and infuse their unique values and goals into the EOT design process. As with all EOTs, the design of the governance system is flexible and ultimately comes down to what works best for each company.

Hummingbird Trust Stewardship Committee and Board of Directors

The transition team determined that Hummingbird Wholesale would have between three and five members of the trust stewardship com-mittee and between three and seven board directors at any given time. For both governing bodies, most members must be current employees of the company. Charlie Tilt also has the option of holding a board and TSC seat for the duration of any seller financing, which under the progressive sale structure is planned to be 10 years. To support communication across governing bodies, the company determined that at least one member of the board of directors should concurrently serve on the TSC.

The founding members of the TSC and board of directors were selected during the transition process. Tilt has a seat on the TSC and serves as the board chair alongside his duties as the company CEO. It is not typically considered a best practice for top management executives to serve as board chairs, and companies should consider how best to balance power at the governance level. In the case of a partial sale, and in some other scenarios, having the CEO and board chair roles held by the same person can be appropriate. Hummingbird employees will elect subsequent TSC members as seats come up for reelection, and the TSC will appoint subsequent boards using a process that Hummingbird Wholesale will crystallize over the first year or two of living its new reality as an EOT company.

Immediately post-transition, the members of the founding governing bodies were tasked with creating several internal policies. Firstly, they needed to define the eligibility criteria, desired qualifications, professional expertise, and other characteristics they desired for employees hoping to participate on the TSC or board of directors. Second, many administrative policies were to be generated and adopted, including a meeting calendar, member/director tracker, agenda protocol, process for minutes and recordkeeping, and process for CEO evaluation. Finally, they needed to determine how elections and appointments will work in the future, including choosing a method for electing new TSC members and appointing new board directors. How a company elects members of the TSC is flexible, and each company needs to define key design decisions on its own. Options for appointing board directors also exist on a spectrum. These areas, like many other EOT design decisions, are areas of flexibility that can be unique to each company's governance ecosystem.

Hummingbird Trust Protector

Hummingbird Wholesale decided to appoint a former employee who is no longer employed at the company as its founding trust protector.

The company felt that the former employee's familiarity and prior experience with the company would be an asset moving forward and that having an external person serve as the TP would remove some possibility for bias in any future grievance processes. In addition to the broad powers outlined in the trust agreement typical of all trust protectors, Hummingbird's trust protector is empowered to approve TSC member compensation, attend regular and special TSC meetings, call special TSC meetings as needed, review TSC minutes and other information related to TSC actions as needed, and approve TSC member removal. In general, trust protectors should consider attending regular and special TSC meetings to stay current on relevant discussion topics and have a line of sight on any burgeoning issues.

Post-transition, Hummingbird Wholesale was tasked with defining a grievance process for escalating matters to the trust protector. Typically, a grievance is presented to the trust protector in writing by the stakeholder alleging the grievance, including a description of the violation as well as a reference to the corresponding sections of the trust agreement. If desired, the company can develop a "grievance form" available to all stakeholders at the company, which can include a description of what constitutes a grievance regarding the trust agreement versus complaints that may fall under the purview of typical company operations. The trust protector will catalog the grievance, send an acknowledgment to the stakeholder submitting the grievance, and determine whether the grievance is legitimate by reviewing it to determine whether the trust's purpose has been violated. The trust protector is responsible for summarizing and communicating findings to the board of directors and trust stewardship committee, cataloging their actions, and taking any further action as needed, depending on the severity of the grievance. In a worst-case scenario, the trust protector is empowered to hire an attorney to bring suit to enforce the trust's purpose.

Creating an Ownership Culture at Hummingbird

At Hummingbird, as at any company transitioning to employee ownership, the first one to three years post-transition have been primarily focused on building the systems and infrastructure necessary for effective stewardship of the company. At Hummingbird Wholesale, transparency around performance was already a large area of focus. The company values information-sharing among all coworkers, and key financial and workplace metrics are shared with employees on a weekly, as well as monthly, basis during staff meetings. Metrics are used to measure outcomes in areas across the company, such as safety, customer service, production, delivery, and inventory, and progress toward goals in each category is shared with employees.

The company is also working to ensure clear communication between the board, the TSC, the trust protector, and the overall employee base. In addition to distinct board and TSC meetings, members of these groups are meeting periodically for one to two years following the company's transition, giving all stakeholders an important line of sight to what their peers are working on, including drafting job descriptions, policies, and handbooks, as well as establishing protocols for effectively running meetings, decision-making, and informing each other as needed on an ongoing basis. It is not necessary for all individuals to be involved in every task, and subcommittees of the board and TSC, or task groups involving members of each group, are encouraged to advance projects as needed.

The company also provides regular updates to employees about what the various governing bodies are working on related to the EOT, and both the board and the TSC are tasked with developing an ongoing communication plan for employees so they can stay abreast of decisions that affect them. In the future, the board and TSC will work to develop bilingual handbooks as well as other educational materials related to the EOT structure that will help educate all coworkers, inform new members of the board and TSC, and drive coworker engagement in the new employee-owned company. These materials are distinct from regular employee handbooks and onboarding, and they are critical to building a culture of ownership.

Conclusion

Growing into an ownership culture is a gradual progression for most EOT companies, even if a strong foundation of transparency and participation already exists before the transition to employee ownership.

Company leaders should be prepared to spend the first one to three years post-transition exploring the best way to make employee ownership work for their company. One of the benefits of the EOT model is its flexibility, and it is important to keep in mind that each company has the ability to refine decisions post-transaction if something does not work well. If company leaders can embrace this period of change while fostering an environment of openness and adaptability, it can go a long way in setting up the company to move through the transition successfully. Other businesses may see little change in day-to-day operations for the first few years as the transition debt is repaid, but once there are profits that can be distributed to employees, that is a key moment to educate employees about the EOT and the role they play in the company's success.

As with any employee-owned company, it takes years of consistent, engaging employee education to build a strong culture of ownership at an EOT. It is vital to create some form of employee education committee tasked with onboarding new employees into the EOT, providing ongoing employee ownership education, and finding opportunities to celebrate this growing but still rare form of company organization that involves and rewards all employees. And some form of open-book management is foundational to connect employees with the most important numbers in the business and engage them in company success.

Resources for Building Ownership Cultures at EOT Companies

- NCEO Ownership Culture Survey (to assess the level of engagement and strategize ways to increase it): https://www.nceo.org/culture/ownership-culture-survey

- NCEO ESOP Communications Sourcebook (can be adapted for communications at an EOT): https://www.nceo.org/ESOP-Communications-Sourcebook/pub.php/id/14

- The Great Game of Business: https://www.greatgame.com/

- DAWI's Practical Guide for Democratic Management: https://www.democraticmanagement.org/ and https://issuu.com/wearedawi/docs/democratic_management_guide_2_1_

CHAPTER 6

Putting the Ownership Back in Employee Ownership Trusts

Corey Rosen

N AN EOT, employees receive a share of the company profits, either as conventional profit sharing or a dividend based on an allocation formula the company creates. But unlike in an employee stock ownership plan (ESOP) or other employee ownership arrangements, the employees have no claim on equity. When they leave, they do not have any shares to cash in. If the company is sold, however, employees would divide the proceeds unless the trust document provides for some other arrangement, such as donating the proceeds to nonprofits (as Oprimax, discussed in the next chapter, does). This lack of an equity stake has raised concerns in the United Kingdom, where EOTs have been the main form of employee ownership since Parliament provided a tax exclusion for selling to an EOT in 2014, that there could be pressure from employees to sell at some point. In the early years, dividends or profit sharing might be relatively low because the acquisition loan is being repaid. Some employees will leave during that process. After the loan is repaid, employees may realize that if the company is sold, they can get a windfall now rather than receive dividends or profit shares over the long term. That could lead to pressure to sell.

Perhaps more importantly, one could argue that if employees only get returns from dividends or profit sharing, they will focus more on the short term. Investments that may not pay off for years but would increase the company's equity value and its competitive advantage might be seen more negatively than if the employees were owners. Actual ownership may also resonate more for employees than profit sharing.

Finding Solutions

People will come down on different sides of this issue, but if ownership does seem important, there are straightforward ways to build it into the EOT model, usually in ways that do not add significant legal or administrative costs. EOT companies can make employees beneficial or actual owners in a few ways:

* *Pair an ESOP with the EOT:* If the purpose of the EOT is to keep the company from being sold rather than to reduce the costs of setting up the plan, an ESOP could own up to 49% of the shares. You can learn more about ESOPs in chapter 1, which compares EOTs to ESOPs.

* *Allow employees to purchase shares:* You could allow employees to buy shares at full price or a discount. Some companies allow employees to designate a portion of their bonus or profit share for this purpose. To avoid costly regulation and disclosure, work with your attorney to structure the plan to avoid securities registration issues. There are several ways to do this.

* *Give employees restricted shares or stock options:* Restricted stock is a grant of a number of shares to an employee subject to a restriction, usually vesting over a few to several years, but profitability or other metrics can be used.

* *Stock options:* The company can grant either incentive stock options (ISOs) or nonqualified stock options (NSOs). ISOs allow the employee to pay capital gains tax on the difference between the grant and sale prices, provided the employee holds the shares for at least one year after exercising and two years after the grant

date. Taxes are due only when the employee sells the shares. NSOs require the employee to pay ordinary income tax on exercise based on the difference between the grant price and the price at exercise, whether the shares are sold or not.

- *Synthetic equity:* Companies can grant the dollar value of a certain number of shares (phantom stock) or the increase in value (stock appreciation rights). The awards are taxable as ordinary income when a payout is made.

In any of these arrangements, companies must have a way to pay the employees the value of the shares. With individual equity awards, employees may have a tax obligation when an award is exercised or vests. If they cannot sell enough shares to at least cover that cost, the award will seem more like a punishment.

The discussion below provides details on options, restricted stock, and synthetic equity.

Stock Options

With stock options, a company grants an employee the right to buy a stated number of shares at a defined grant price. The options vest over a period of time or once certain individual, group, or corporate goals are met. Companies can choose whatever vesting rules they want. Vesting rules do not have to be the same for each employee, although they usually are. Vesting applies to each option grant—it is not cumulative as in an ESOP or other retirement plan. Some companies set time-based vesting schedules but allow options to vest sooner if performance goals are met. Once vested, the employee can exercise the option at the grant price at any time over the option term up to the expiration date. For instance, the company may grant an employee options to buy 1,000 shares at $10 per share. The options vest 25% per year over four years and have a term of 10 years. If the stock goes up, the employee will pay $10 per share to buy the stock. The difference between the $10 grant price and the exercise price is the "spread." If the stock goes to $25 after seven years, and the employee exercises all options, the spread will be $15 per share.

Kinds of Options

Options are either incentive stock options (ISOs) or nonqualified stock options (NSOs), which are sometimes referred to as nonstatutory stock options. When an employee exercises an NSO, the spread on exercise is taxable to the employee as ordinary income, even if the shares are not yet sold. A corresponding amount is deductible by the company. There is no legally required holding period for the shares after exercising, although the company may impose one. Any subsequent gain or loss on the shares after exercising is taxed as a capital gain or loss when the employee sells the shares.

An ISO enables an employee to (1) defer taxation on the option from the date of exercise until the date of sale of the underlying shares and (2) pay taxes on their entire gain at capital gains rates rather than ordinary income tax rates. Certain conditions must be met to qualify for ISO treatment:

1. The employee must hold the stock for at least one year after the exercise date and two years after the grant date.

2. An ISO can be first exercisable only for up to $100,000 of stock in any calendar year, as measured by the stock's fair market value on the grant date. It means that only $100,000 in grant price value can become eligible for exercise in any year. If there is overlapping vesting, such as if options are granted annually and vest gradually, companies must track outstanding ISOs to ensure the amounts that become vested under different grants to the same person will not exceed $100,000 in value in any year. Any portion of an ISO grant that exceeds the limit is treated as an NSO.

3. The exercise price must not be less than the market price of the company's stock on the grant date.

4. Only employees can qualify for ISOs.

5. The option must be granted under a written plan that shareholders have approved, specifies how many shares can be issued under the plan under ISOs, and identifies the class of employees eligible to receive the options.

6. Options must be granted within 10 years of the date of the board of directors' adoption of the plan.

7. The option must be exercised within 10 years of the grant date.

8. If, at the time of grant, the employee owns more than 10% of the voting power of all outstanding stock of the company, the ISO exercise price must be at least 110% of the market value of the stock on that date and may not have a term of more than five years.

If all the rules for ISOs are met, then the eventual sale of the shares is called a "qualifying disposition," and the employee pays long-term capital gains tax on the total increase in value between the grant price and the sale price. The company does not take a tax deduction when there is a qualifying disposition.

If, however, the ISO rules are not met, most often because the employee exercises and sells the shares before meeting the required holding periods, there is a "disqualifying disposition," and the spread on exercise is taxable to the employee at ordinary income tax rates. Any increase or decrease in the shares' value between exercise and sale is taxed at capital gains rates (which will be short- or long-term based on how long the shares are held). In this instance, the company may deduct the spread on exercise.

If an employee exercises ISOs and does not sell the underlying shares by the end of the year, the spread on the option at exercise is a "preference item" for purposes of the alternative minimum tax (AMT). So even though the shares may not have been sold, the exercise requires the employee to add back the gain on exercise and other AMT preference items to see whether an alternative minimum tax payment is due.

In contrast to ISOs, NSOs can be issued to anyone—employees, directors, consultants, suppliers, customers, etc. There are no special tax benefits for NSOs, however. Like an ISO, there is no tax on the grant of the option, but when it is exercised, the spread between the grant and exercise price is taxable as ordinary income. The company receives a corresponding tax deduction.

Exercising an Option

There are several ways to exercise a stock option, but at an EOT company, the most practical would be for the employee to purchase the shares at the grant price, receive the shares at whatever the higher value the shares are at exercise, and then sell them at some point. This raises a tricky issue. The employee is using money that has already been taxed to buy shares, but the shares may not be liquid unless the company is sold (generally not what an EOT wants to do) or the company buys them back. With an NSO, the employee also has an immediate tax obligation on the spread. If the option is an ISO, taxes can be delayed until the employee sells the shares, but this must occur no sooner than one year after the exercise date and two years after the grant date.

If the company buys back the shares immediately, an NSO functions similarly to a stock appreciation right (SAR), described below. Because SARs are simpler and involve no actual shares, they are probably a better choice for an EOT. However, ISOs could be valuable for employees in a high enough tax bracket so that their ordinary income tax rate is higher than their capital gains rate, which generally is true for employees making six figures.

Accounting

Under the applicable accounting rules for equity compensation (Accounting Standards Codification Topic 718), companies must use an option-pricing model to calculate the present value of all option awards as of the grant date and show this as an expense on their income statements. The expense recognized should be adjusted based on vesting experience (so unvested shares do not count as a charge to compensation).

Restricted Stock

Restricted stock is the grant of shares or the right to buy shares to employees subject to some restriction, generally a vesting requirement. When employees are awarded restricted stock, they have the right to make what is called a Section 83(b) election. If they make the election, they are taxed at ordinary income tax rates on the "bargain element" of the award at the time of grant. If the shares were simply granted to the employee, then the bargain element is their full value. If some consideration is paid, then the tax is based on the difference between what is paid and the fair market value at the time of the grant. If the full price is paid, there is no tax. Any future change in the value of the shares between the filing and the sale is then taxed as a capital gain or loss, not ordinary income. An employee who does not make an 83(b) election must pay ordinary income taxes on the difference between the amount paid for the shares and their fair market value when the restrictions lapse. Subsequent changes in value are capital gains or losses. Employees are not allowed to make Section 83(b) elections for restricted stock units, as discussed below.

The employer gets a tax deduction only for amounts on which employees must pay income taxes, regardless of whether a Section 83(b) election is made. A Section 83(b) election carries some risk. If the employee makes the election and pays tax, but the restrictions never lapse, the employee does not get the taxes paid refunded, nor does the employee get the shares.

Restricted stock accounting parallels option accounting in most respects. If the only restriction is time-based vesting, companies account for restricted stock by determining the total compensation cost when the award is made. However, no option-pricing model is used. If the employee is simply given 1,000 restricted shares worth $10 per share, then a $10,000 cost is recognized. If the employee buys the shares at fair value, no charge is recorded; if there is a discount, that counts as a cost. The cost is then amortized over the period of vesting until the restrictions lapse. Because the accounting is based on the initial cost, companies with low share prices will find that a vesting requirement for the award means their accounting expense will be very low.

If vesting is contingent on performance, then the company estimates when the performance goal is likely to be achieved and recognizes the expense over the expected vesting period. If the performance condition is not based on stock price movements, the amount recognized is adjusted for awards that are not expected to vest or never do vest; if it is based on stock price movements, it is not adjusted to reflect awards that are not expected to or do not vest.

Restricted stock units (RSUs) provide that the employee will get the shares only once they are vested. The employee cannot make an 83(b) election on RSUs and is taxed on the award when shares are distributed, typically at vesting.

Phantom Stock and Stock Appreciation Rights

If employees who get stock options or restricted stock cash them in when they vest or soon after, there may not be much point in using these awards instead of synthetic equity, i.e., phantom stock or stock appreciation rights (SARs). They provide the equivalent financial value without the added paperwork of shares. Options or restricted stock have the potential advantage of allowing the employee to take capital gains treatment on the gains made from the awards. However, this is valuable only to relatively high-income filers for whom capital gains rates are meaningfully lower than ordinary income tax rates.

The two forms of synthetic equity, SARs and phantom stock, are very similar concepts. Both essentially are bonus plans that grant not stock but rather the right to receive an award based on the value of the company's stock, hence the terms "appreciation rights" and "phantom." SARs typically provide the employee with a cash or stock payment based on the increase in the value of a stated number of shares over a specific period. Phantom stock provides a cash or stock bonus based on the value of a stated number of shares, to be paid at the end of a specified period. SARs may not have a specific settlement date; as with options, the employee may have flexibility in choosing when to exercise the SAR. Phantom stock may offer dividend equivalent payments; SARs would not.

When the payout is made, the value of the award is taxed as ordinary income to the employee and is deductible to the employer. Some phantom plans condition the receipt of the award on meeting certain objectives, such as sales, profits, or other targets. These plans often refer to their phantom stock as "performance units."

Phantom stock and SARs can be given to anyone, but if they are given out broadly to employees and designed to pay out upon termination, there is a possibility that they will be considered retirement plans under the Employee Retirement Income Security Act of 1974 (ERISA) and will be subject to ERISA's rules. Paying out periodically can avoid this problem.

Some companies settle these awards in stock. In that case, when an employee fully vests, the company provides actual shares instead of their cash value. To avoid tax problems for employees, the company will provide enough funds for employees to pay taxes and then give the employees however many additional shares the remaining dollars can purchase. At an EOT company, this has value only if the company is sold or later provides liquidity for the shares.

Because SARs and phantom plans are essentially cash bonuses, companies need to figure out how to pay for them. Even if awards are paid in shares, employees will want to sell the shares, at least in sufficient amounts to pay their taxes. Does the company just make a promise to pay, or does it really put aside the funds? If the award is paid in stock, is there a market for the stock? If it is only a promise, will employees believe the benefit is as phantom as the stock? If it is in real funds set aside for this purpose, the company will put after-tax dollars aside instead of using those dollars for the business. The fund can also be subject to excess accumulated earnings tax.

Phantom stock and cash-settled SARs are subject to liability accounting, meaning the accounting costs associated with them are not settled until they pay out or expire. For cash-settled SARs, the compensation expense for awards is estimated each quarter using an option-pricing model and then trued up when the SAR is settled; for phantom stock, the underlying value is calculated each quarter and trued up through the final settlement date. Phantom stock is treated in the same way as deferred cash compensation.

In contrast, if a SAR is settled in stock, then the accounting treatment is the same as for an option. The company must record the fair value of the award at grant and recognize expense ratably over the expected service period. If the award is performance-vested, the company must estimate how long it will take to meet the goal. If the performance measurement is tied to the company's stock price, an option-pricing model must be used to determine whether and when the goal will be met.

Creating Rules for Equity Grant Programs

When providing options, restricted stock, phantom stock, or stock appreciation rights, companies need to set up rules for who gets what and when, and how much they should get.

First, you need to decide who is eligible. Will it be all employees, only employees meeting a minimum service requirement (such as 1,000 hours in a calendar year), only employees who meet some performance target, or some other rule? A sensible approach would be to follow the same eligibility rules you have for participation in the dividends from the trust.

Second, you need to choose a vesting method and schedule. Most companies use tenure-based vesting over a few years, generally on a graduated basis, such as 20% per year. The vesting normally applies to each award. Say Mary gets an award in 2024 that has three-year graduated vesting. She fully vests for the 2024 award in 2027. If she gets an award in 2025, that award does not fully vest until 2028. A company could, however, simply say that Mary gets vesting credit for all the prior years she has served since the first grant for each subsequent grant. In that case, her 2025 award would also vest in 2027, and a grant in 2027 would be fully vested. This vesting approach parallels how vesting works in an ESOP or a 401(k) plan. You could, however, make vesting contingent on company performance, personal performance, or a combination of both ("We must reach X revenues, and you must have been here Y years," for instance).

Third, you need to decide when the award pays out. As noted above, if the awards pay out only at termination or upon a corporate change of control, the plan can be deemed a retirement plan covered by ERISA, which would impose substantial compliance issues similar to what an ESOP would be required to do. Paying out every few years avoids this problem. The payout, of course, requires liquidity.

Fourth, you need to decide how large the equity pool will be and how it will be divided. One approach is just to pick some percentage—10%, 20%, or whatever seems comfortable. A problem with this approach is that when you have used up the pool, you now have to figure out how to reward new employees. An alternative is to set a goal (profits, revenue, or some other target). If the goal is met, some percentage of the excess can be reserved for the equity pool that year. That way, the pool grows only if the company does, and it gives employees another reason to work to meet the target.

To divide up the pool, companies can use any number of formulas, but the most common would be giving everyone the same percentage, basing allocations on relative pay (as in ESOPs), basing allocations on merit, or using a point formula giving credit for some of each.

Conclusion

Making employees actual owners can help keep the company's focus on the long term while providing a source of wealth beyond dividends, goals worth considering for an EOT company. We welcome you to contact the NCEO to discuss these ideas further.

CHAPTER 7

EOT Case Studies

Corey Rosen

ACP International

ACP International is an Arlington, Texas-based manufacturer of a variety of tags, signs, street signs, markers, and decals. Its customers include cable and utility companies, schools, cities, and other users. ACP now occupies a 72,000-square-foot facility. ACP founder Joe Nussbaum always took pride in how employees were treated, resulting in exceptional tenure rates among ACP's 57 employees. When he started to think about business transition, selling to another company or any other buyer who would not retain this approach just was not appealing.

Nussbaum told attendees of the NCEO's 2023 Fall Forum that he looked at doing an ESOP. While the tax benefits were appealing, the costs of doing an EOT would be in the range of $60,000 to $100,000, while doing an ESOP would cost as much as five times more. For a company ACP's size, the extra cost, complexity, ongoing costs, and rules just did not justify the tax benefits.

Nussbaum also worried that adopting an ESOP could force the company to be sold at some point. ESOP fiduciary rules require that the ESOP trustee and company board give serious consideration to an offer at a significant premium, generally at least 30% and probably 50% or more. While there are a variety of ways to legitimately discourage would-be buyers, and while ESOP companies are very rarely sold when they do not want to be, an EOT can be set up so that a sale can only happen under specifically defined circumstances.

ACP converted to EOT ownership in 2022. No formal third-party valuation was required. Instead, Nussbaum hired someone to do a very low-cost informal valuation. A perpetual purpose trust (PPT) was created to buy all the shares. Nussbaum took a seven-year promissory note to finance the sale. He remains the CEO. While the note remains pending, profits above a required minimum level will only be used to pay off the note; once the note is paid off, a profit-sharing plan will be set up.

The PPT has an independent trustee (the attorney who set up their plan) who monitors the actions of the company board of directors only concerning the purposes of the trust, not issues related to managing the company. Currently, the ACP board consists of five directors. Four directors are employee-owners and are called inside directors, and one is a former employee. All directors have the same roles and responsibilities, except that the outside director has the additional role of doing an annual payroll evaluation. Over time, Nussbaum expects to add independent outside directors if they can bring relevant experience and a fresh perspective.

A sale of the company is permitted only if these three conditions are met:

1. The board believes an offer is 25% above fair market value.

2. The majority of the board approves a sale.

3. The majority of employee-owners approve a sale.

Nussbaum stated:

> What I noticed over and over, much more often than not, is that after a couple of years, the only winner in a deal to sell to an outside buyer was the previous owner's wallet. The employees fared poorly. The customers were less satisfied. Vendor relationships were less fruitful. Even the buyers didn't financially benefit like they thought they would. The previous owner's wallet may have been fat, but often, their heart was broken. I didn't want that for my company; I wanted our employees, customers, and vendors to thrive. After all, they were a part of building the company, just as I was. I believe a company should operate in a way that is good

for every party: employees, owners, vendors, and customers. Employee ownership offers a good opportunity for that. Finally, there is great joy in seeing people grow and achieve things they never thought they could do. With employee ownership, I get to see a lot of people experience this opportunity.

Paras and Associates

Created in 2006 in Emeryville, CA, Paras and Associates describes itself as "the only provider of interpreter systems that enables hospitals to share interpreter resources with other hospitals within the Health Care Interpreter Network." Paras provides a video interpreting platform that healthcare systems and a few other users use to allow their interpreters sitting in a call center to broadcast their interpreting capabilities throughout their hospital system. Paras was founded not to make profits but to do social good. The difficulty some patients have in communicating with and understanding their healthcare professionals significantly affects health outcomes for these patients. Paras was dedicated to creating a more cost-effective way to make these interactions more productive.

Paras now has 10 employees. Melinda Paras and her co-owners looked at selling to a competitor, but that struck them as a terrible idea, one that would not be likely to maintain the culture and values the founders had created. They heard about ESOPs and initially thought that was the only alternative for transitioning to employee ownership. For a company their size, however, the costs were unreasonably high, and the rules for retirement plans were too complex. When they learned about EOTs, that seemed like a practical alternative.

The company hired an appraiser to determine fair market value, and the sale was financed through a seller note paid off over 10 years to the owners. The company has had a board of directors from the outset consisting of four to five staff members, including the CFO, the CEO, and the chief technology officer. That continues under the EOT. The board determines how much of the company's annual profits will go into the profit-sharing pool. The board cannot decide to allocate all the profits to themselves. Instead, profits are allocated based on relative pay, which at Paras is fairly flat compared to similar companies. There is a trustee whose responsibility is limited and does not involve managing the company. The trustee's primary duty is to make sure the goals of the trust are preserved. That includes any decision to sell the company, which can be based only on a conclusion that the social and employment goals of the company would be maintained. Paras has veto power over a decision to sell.

Paras says:

> I think the first thing that drew me to [the EOT] is that there was an immediate value to the employees. In an ESOP, the employees don't really see the value of their shares in the ESOP until they retire. It's really a retirement plan essentially, and as they leave the company, then they get paid for their stocks, for their ownership portion. In the employee ownership trust model, the employees receive a profit share at the end of every fiscal year, which means that they see the immediate result of becoming an employee-owner. In our model, we decided to distribute the profits to the employees based on their salary proportions. So if we're giving out $100,000 in profits to the employees, it will be divided based on salaries. That way, those who have more responsibility and greater leadership in the company, who have higher salaries, are going to get a little bit more of the profits than others. But frankly, the distance between our lowest-paid employee and our highest-paid employee is not that high, so frankly, it's pretty good sharing of the profit.

Optimax

Located in Ontario, NY, Optimax was started in 1991 based on innovative research that came out of the University of Rochester funded by Kodak and Texas Instruments. Optimax formed as a new company to adopt this technology. They manufacture high-precision optics for aerospace, defense, and semiconductor industries. It has grown its capabilities to include innovative research, optical coatings, and engineered solutions. It is America's largest precision optics manufacturer and now has nearly 500 employees.

CEO Rick Plympton and his business partner, Mike Mandina, spent five years looking for a way to deal with business transition that was financially practical and, most importantly, retained the company's values and culture. They considered a sale to an ESOP, but one of Plympton's concerns was that an ESOP company could be sold and, if the offer were considerably over fair market value, in some circumstances would *have* to be sold. He was also concerned that an ESOP would mean that employees' financial well-being would be at risk if the company fell on hard times. In 2020, they decided an EOT would be the best fit. The primary objectives for the succession plan were to make sure the company would not be sold, that at least 25% of the profits would be distributed annually to employees, and that there was a platform that would set the stage for future growth for many decades.

The pair gifted part of their ownership to the trust, and the rest was sold back to Optimax through a 5-year seller note, followed by a second tranche for their remaining equity on a 10-year note. One-quarter of annual profit is set aside to repay the note (meaning it could be repaid sooner than 15 years). Between paying off the seller notes and the monthly employee profit sharing, Plympton believes about 25% percent of profits will be available for growth, but that will rise to 50% when the notes are repaid.

Optimax developed a phantom stock option plan for key leaders, in which the shares vest over five years. There are also Class B non-voting, dividend-paying shares that selected leadership employees can buy. These shares can be cashed in as well, but typically on a longer time horizon than phantom stock options.

Optimax has always had a very high-engagement culture. Leah Hamilton, who oversees culture at the company, says that knowing the company will not be sold creates a psychological sense of ownership and security. That is especially true given that Optimax's growth and market position could make it an attractive target for acquisition, in which case it is unlikely that the acquiring company would retain the company's culture and compensation philosophy.

The company has always been very open-book, sharing both overall financial numbers and a variety of key performance metrics. Profits are shared monthly and distributed equally across the company. The janitor gets the same bonus check as a company officer. The company also has a 401(k) plan that is funded generously with the goal of every employee with 30 years or more of tenure having the ability to retire as a millionaire.

The trust is designed as a perpetual purpose trust. The company cannot be sold other than for solvency issues, in which case any remaining funds from the sale of the company would go to nonprofits in the community. The trust is governed by Optimax's two founders plus one employee who is responsible for representing the workforce on the trustee board. Its sole purpose is to carry out the terms of the trust by ensuring profit sharing with employees, rejecting offers to buy the company, and ensuring that company leadership is doing things to create market solutions through innovation and create more jobs to strengthen its community.

In 2021, celebrating Optimax's 30th anniversary, Plympton noted that Optimax had grown from a startup to more than 400 employees and about $500 million in revenue, half of that being shared with employees through payroll, benefits, and bonuses. In the next 30 years, with conservative growth, Optimax will generate more than $5 billion in revenue, roughly half of which will be shared with employees, providing financial security for families and strengthening its community.

ABOUT THE AUTHORS

Anne-Claire Broughton is the principal of Broughton Consulting, LLC, a certified B corporation that helps organizations engage employees at all levels for business success through open-book management, employee ownership, and healthy organizational cultures. Broughton assists business owners with succession planning via employee ownership (ESOPs, worker cooperatives, and employee ownership trusts). She is an open-book management coach with The Great Game of Business, empowering teams to understand and influence the most important numbers. Broughton is the founder and board vice chair of the North Carolina Employee Ownership Center, and she previously spent more than 13 years advising early-stage businesses as a cofounder and senior director of SJF Institute. Publications include "The Human Capital Advantage: A Curriculum for Early Stage Ventures" (with the Hitachi Foundation); the Business Action Guide series on innovative employee engagement practices (with the Hitachi Foundation); "Employees Matter: Maximizing Company Value Through Workforce Engagement," which profiles 24 companies that can link their progressive employee practices with improved bottom-line results; "Embracing Open Book Management to Fuel Employee Engagement and Corporate Sustainability" (with UNC Kenan-Flagler Business School); and "Beyond Paycheck-to-Paycheck: Wealth Building Strategies for Venture Capital Funds to use with Portfolio Companies and Their Employees."

Courtney Kemp is a senior client services manager at Project Equity. She works to counsel small business owners on preserving their businesses via employee ownership, guiding selling owners as well as employees through employee ownership feasibility studies and transitions, and supporting businesses that have recently transitioned to employee ownership. At Project Equity, she specializes in employee ownership trust transitions and contributes to the program management of the organization's capital initiatives to finance employee ownership transitions for small businesses nationwide. Courtney has an MA in development policy and an MBA in social finance and impact management from Middlebury College.

Alison Lingane is the cofounder and chief innovation and investment officer at Project Equity, where she founded and manages the Employee Ownership Catalyst Fund. She has dedicated her career to enabling business to be a force for good. Before launching Project Equity, Alison held executive roles at mission-driven businesses that are designed to have human impact at scale. She brings those scaling lessons back full circle to her work at Project Equity, turning businesses into community change agents through employee ownership. Alison has been recognized by many fellowship invitations, and she and her cofounder Hilary Abell received the Heinz Award for the Economy in 2022. Alison holds a BS from Harvard University and an MBA from UC Berkeley's Haas School of Business.

Christopher Michael is responsible for developing the employee ownership trust as a new financial and legal mechanism in the U.S. and has published articles introducing the concept in leading peer-reviewed journals, including *Tax Notes* and *Probate & Property*. He is also a professor at Rutgers University, where he is a director of the Institute for the Study of Employee Ownership and Profit Sharing. Chris holds a BA from Columbia University and a JD/PhD from the City University of New York, where he spent a decade researching the economic, historical, and legal foundations of employee ownership and authored a book manuscript on the economic history of employee-owned businesses.

Corey Rosen is the NCEO's founder and former executive director and now is its senior staff member. Corey has spoken on various subjects related to employee ownership all over the world with government, business, and union leaders, and he is regularly quoted in leading magazines and newspapers. He has appeared on national television and radio programs and also has authored four books on employee ownership, plus more than 100 articles for various business, academic, and professional publications. He has authored or coauthored several of the NCEO's practical and research publications. He holds a PhD in political science from Cornell University.

Stacey Smith is the vice president, programs at Project Equity, where she manages the teams focused on engaging business owners, their advisors, and key employees to implement employee ownership transitions. She began her career as a CPA and went on to build consulting teams in the private and nonprofit sectors focused on using business as a force for positive impact in society. She worked for over 15 years in the ESG and corporate sustainability field. She is now a recognized thought leader on employee ownership transitions. She holds a B.S. in business administration and has completed multiple executive education programs in change management, organizational learning, sustainability, and employee ownership.

Steve Virgil is a professor at Wake Forest University School of Law in North Carolina, where he teaches business law and leads a clinical program that advises startups and social enterprises. He has published many articles and two books on business and community development. In his law practice, Steve advises clients on creating employee ownership trusts and converting closely held businesses to worker-owned cooperatives as a succession strategy. He regularly works with clients to create strategies that align with their vision.

The National Center for Employee Ownership (NCEO) is a nonprofit organization that has supported the employee ownership community since 1981. Our mission is to help employee ownership thrive. We have more than 3,000 members because we help people make smart decisions about employee ownership, with everything from reliable information on technical issues to helping companies reach the full potential of employee ownership.

We generate original research, facilitate the exchange of best practices at our live and online events, feature the best and most current writing by experts in our publications, and help employee ownership companies build ownership cultures where employees think and act like owners.

Membership Benefits

NCEO members receive the following benefits and more:

- The members-only newsletter *Employee Ownership Report.*
- Access to the NCEO's members-only website resources, including the Document Library, ESOP Q&A, multiple tookits, and more.
- Free access to both live and recorded webinars.
- Discounts on books and other NCEO products and services.
- The right to contact the NCEO for answers to questions.

To join as a member or order publications, visit our website at www.nceo.org. Visit us at www.nceo.org/r/eot to order this book.

Printed in Great Britain
by Amazon

41001258R00056